T0384945

ROUTLEDGE LIBRARY EDITIONS:
LOGIC

Volume 20

THE LOGIC OF
COMMANDS

THE LOGIC OF COMMANDS

NICHOLAS RESCHER

Routledge
Taylor & Francis Group

LONDON AND NEW YORK

First published in 1966 by Routledge & Kegan Paul Ltd

This edition first published in 2020
by Routledge
2 Park Square, Milton Park, Abingdon, Oxon OX14 4RN

and by Routledge
52 Vanderbilt Avenue, New York, NY 10017

Routledge is an imprint of the Taylor & Francis Group, an informa business

British Library Cataloguing in Publication Data
A catalogue record for this book is available from the British Library

ISBN: 978-0-367-41707-9 (Set)
ISBN: 978-0-367-81582-0 (Set) (ebk)
ISBN: 978-0-367-42256-1 (Volume 20) (hbk)
ISBN: 978-0-367-85432-4 (Volume 20) (ebk)

Publisher's Note
The publisher has gone to great lengths to ensure the quality of this reprint but points out that some imperfections in the original copies may be apparent.

Disclaimer
The publisher has made every effort to trace copyright holders and would welcome correspondence from those they have been unable to trace.

THE LOGIC OF
COMMANDS

BY

Nicholas Rescher

LONDON: Routledge & Kegan Paul Ltd
NEW YORK: Dover Publications Inc.

First published 1966
in Great Britain by
Routledge & Kegan Paul Ltd
Broadway House, 68–74 Carter Lane
London, E.C.4
and in the U.S.A. by
Dover Publications Inc.
180 Varick Street
New York, 10014

Printed in Great Britain

Its author dedicates the book to his friend and
colleague of long standing

ADOLF GRÜNBAUM

'Begin at the beginning, and go on till you come to the end: then stop.'

The King of Hearts to the White Rabbit

CONTENTS

Contents

Contents

Contents

PREFACE

Although the logic of commands has attracted much attention in recent years, this has in large measure been by way of controversy regarding fundamentals. It is not a finished discipline, but one that is 'in the making'. This fact that seems to me to endow it with particular interest and desert for attention.

Although the present treatment of commands is intended to provide a 'logical theory' of commands in the most orthodox sense of the term, it has turned out in the event that certain rather unorthodox items of machinery had to be deployed in the interests of moving towards this objective. Useful tools have been found ready-made to our purpose in such diverse items as the concept of a 'scenario' in operations research and the technique of 'flow diagram' construction in computer programming. I make no apology for bringing these seemingly strange bedfellows together here — this too contributes to the interest of the enterprise.

I acknowledge with thanks the helpful comments and criticisms of my Pittsburgh students Bas van Fraassen and Richard K. Martin and colleagues Storrs McCall and John Robison on early drafts of the material presented here. Exchanges of ideas with Ernest Sosa, now of Brown University, who wrote a

Preface

doctoral dissertation on the logic of commands under my direction, contributed helpfully at many points. Discussion with André Gombay of McGill University provided several ideas — in particular the antilogistic justification of command inferences with assertoric conclusions. I also thank Professor Herbert A. Simon of the Carnegie Institute of Technology for helpful comments. Miss Dorothy Henle gave efficient service in preparing the difficult typescript for the printer and helped to see the book through the press. Mr. Stephen E. Norris helped to check the proofs and did the bulk of the work in preparing the indices. Above all, I owe a great debt to my friend and colleague Nuel D. Belnap, Jr. for the stimulus of provocative and helpful discussion of numerous points.

N.R.

Pittsburgh
August 1964

xii

Chapter One

INTRODUCTION

1.1. Imperatives and Commands. The aim of this book is to present the fundamentals of a logical theory of commands. In large measure it is devoted to a task preliminary to any adequate articulation of such a theory — the clarification of the basic constituent ideas required for a viable analysis of the complex concept of a command. Only when our feet have been set securely upon the firm ground of an appropriate conceptual clarification can a meaningful study of logical mechanisms get under way.

The topic which engages our attention here is frequently treated under the heading of the 'logic of imperatives'. But this is not strictly correct. Imperatives (like indicatives) form a wide *grammatical* category; commands (like assertions) represent a rather narrower *functional* grouping. Imperatives can be used to give counsel or advice (unconditionally, as with 'Ask your doctor about it!', or conditionally as with 'If you want to make sure of that, ask your attorney about it!'), to upbraid or reproach ('Don't ever advise me again!'), to denounce ('Go to the devil!'), to implore aid or to request co-operation ('Save me: I'm drowning!'), to make prayers and

1

supplications ('Give us this day our daily bread!'). They can even — in the case of conditional imperatives — be used to make a purely factual assertion ('If you want to visit the tallest structure in Pittsburgh, visit the Gulf Oil Building!' adds really nothing to 'The Gulf Building is the tallest structure in Pittsburgh'[1]). Laws of nature are sometimes formulated as hypothetical imperatives — for example 'If you want water to freeze, cool it to 32°F!' in place of the direct 'Water freezes at 32°F'.

We shall here deal only with *commands* (construing this term broadly to include orders, directives, injunctions, instructions, and prohibitions or 'negative' commands[2]), and even this only in part. The particular way in which we are concerned with commands needs further specification in certain respects which will be indicated below. Although considerations of precision may ultimately lead us into certain departures from 'ordinary language', it is our purpose to develop a theory of 'commands' in the sense of the everyday use of the relevant concepts.

---

[1] For just this point about certain 'hypothetical imperatives' see *Hare* (1952), p. 34. [All references of this author-plus-date form refer to the *Bibliography* appended at the end of this book.]

[2] There are substantial analogies between the locution '*X* commands *Y* to do *A*' on the one hand, and the locutions '*X*'s requests *Y* to do *A*' and '*X* urges *Y* to do *A* (i.e., recommends that he do *A*)' and '*X* authorizes (permits) *Y* to do *A*', on the other. Compare *Wellman* (1961), pp. 230–235. Many points of the logic of commands can be carried over to the logic of requests, recommendations, and authorizations, but we shall not explore such kinships here.

2

Introduction

1.2. The Key Problem. While a great many interesting issues arise within the rather wide area of a 'logic of commands', one problem above all lies at the focus of our interest here. It is this: Can one articulate appropriate concepts of *inference* and of *validity* in such a way as to legitimate the inference of a command conclusion from premises consisting of other commands (and also possibly including assertoric statements)? This question of the prospects for 'valid inference' among commands is on our conception of the matter the key problem of the logical theory of commands.

The concept of validity, although it is our main objective, is not actually dealt with overtly until halfway through the book — it is broached in Chapter Seven, to be precise. The reason is simply that (as the White Rabbit explains to the King of Hearts) 'There's a great deal to come before that!' The inquiry begins with a general examination of the conceptual structure of commands (in Chapter Two), and then goes on to build up (in Chapters Three through Five) the necessary terminology, symbolism, and ideographic and conceptual machinery needed for the ensuing formal discussion. Chapter Six is transitional and preparatory — it introduces the auxiliary concept of 'coverage' of a command by one or more others. This concept gives the paradigm of validity which serves as basis for the development of the conception of validity finally presented in Chapter Seven and developed thereafter. The larger issues of a logic of commands can be dealt with in a fruitful and straightforward way only after the necessary groundwork has been prepared.

1.3. Why a 'Logic of Commands'? Quite apart from whatever *intrinsic* interest a logical theory of commands may possess, it seems worthwhile from two *external* perspectives. Firstly, it cannot but help to shed the light of contrast upon the logical theory of purely assertoric statements. Secondly, the inquiry will possess an instrumental value for ethics, where the notion of *commanding* cannot but play a role. Indeed various recent writers on ethics — R. M. Hare, in particular — have tried to conjure with commands and imperatives, and have tried to base far-reaching conclusions in ethical theory upon considerations regarding them. (We shall have occasion to consider below the particularly interesting stratagem of Henri Poincaré.)

Wittgenstein somewhere spoke of a discussion as suffering from a deficiency disease caused by a too restricted diet of examples. The theory of commands has been the victim of a deceptive appearance of triviality because much of the literature confines itself to rather simple minded stock examples of the 'John, close the window!' type. The more complicated cases of the sort to be found in legal contexts (e.g., instructions to the executors of wills), in examination instructions, and in computer programs, for example, are generally neglected. Our present treatment of the subject will try to free itself of this defect, and will take its inspiration primarily from the last-named area.

In ordinary life, the instructions one is given are generally simple and straightforward — we can get by with simple 'common sense' and do not require anything sufficiently formal and formidable to deserve the name of a *logic*. And yet we do 'reason' from commands and sets of commands. And we would surely be prepared to say that the examination instructions:

> Write the answer to every question you select on a single sheet!
> Answer no fewer than three nor more than four questions!

would 'imply' the instruction: 'Write no more than four sheets for the entire examination!' Or again we would surely be prepared to class as 'self-inconsistent' the set of instructions consisting of the aforementioned two with the addition of: 'Write your examination on exactly two sheets!' Or (to take yet another intuitively plausible example) if we have an instruction manual that reads:

> Whenever condition C is realized, take course of action A!
> Never take course of action A unless you first do B!

we would want to say that these two instructions are 'equivalent' with:

> Whenever condition C is realized, do B first and then take course of action A!

1.4. Historical Observations. The logical theory of commands is widely regarded as a very new and 'non-classical' branch of logic. We know, however, that it — like the logic of questions — occupied the attention of one of the great logical schools of antiquity, that of the Stoics. Diogenes Laertius reports in his list of the logical works of Chrysippus (280–209 B.C.) that this important Stoic logician wrote a treatise 'On Commands' (*Peri prostagmatōn*) in two books[3].

The founding father of the logical theory of commands in modern times is Ernst Mally. His *Grundgesetze des Sollens: Elemente der Logik des Willens* (Graz, 1926) is the groundbreaking work not only in the logic of commands but in deontic logic as well[4]. Its defects notwithstanding (and they are real, but easily exaggerated) Mally's pioneering efforts represents an outstanding contribution to applied logic[5].

More recent interest in the logic of imperatives received its initial impetus during the latter 1930's in the wake of the logical positivists' insistence upon the exclusive meaningfulness of factual assertions, and the consequent problem of attempting assertoric treatment of other types of *prima facie* non-assertoric statements such as imperatives[6]. The problem was especially acute for the positivists, because commands, far from being

---

[3] *Lives of Eminent Philosophers*, 7: 191; ed. D. H. Hicks in the Loeb series, vol. 2, p. 300. Compare B. Mates, *Stoic Logic* (Berkeley, 1953), p. 19.

[4] Mally even coined the word *Deontik* as name for the '*Logik des Willens*' he was attempting to devise. Mally's contribution to the logic of commands is concisely outlined in *Menger* (1939), pp. 57–58.

[5] Mally's work on commands culminates — but goes far beyond — discussions of this topic by Franz Brentano and others in his tradition, preeminently Brentano's pupil Alexis Meinong, who was Mally's teacher. For details see the *Bibliography*.

[6] Imperatives gained special prominence because the positivists tended (under Kantian influence) to regard moral rules as imperatives. Thus Carnap maintained (*Philosophy and Logical Syntax* [London, 1935], p. 23) that there is only a matter of stylistic difference of formulation between 'Killing is evil' and 'Do not kill!'

6

'nonsense', can serve as basis for apparently rigorous reasonings: 'Put all the blue boxes on the table; this box is blue: put this box on the table!' The situation is helpfully summarized in a brief quote from a paper on 'Imperatives and Logic' published by Alf Ross over two decades ago (1944):

> The problems of this treatise are in line with those which have, as far as I know, been first propounded by Walter Dubislaw in his treatise 'Zur Unbegründbarkeit der Forderungssätze' [published] in *Theoria*, 1937. Since then Jørgen Jørgensen, Grelling, Grue-Sørensen, Hofstadter and McKinsey, and Rose Rand have treated similar problems[7]. The problem has not been delimited in the same way by these authors, but their object has always been to elucidate whether sentences which are not descriptive [i.e., factual], but which express a demand, a wish, or the like, may be made objects of logical treatment in the same or a similar manner as the indicative sentences[8].

Although a great deal has been written on the logic of imperatives generally and of commands in particular in the years since the initial revival of the subject in the later 1930's, it is, I think, only fair to say that there is virtually no single issue in the field upon which a settled consensus has been reached. Indeed a significant fraction of the literature consists of attempts to call into question the very possibility of the subject itself[9].

[7] For detailed citations see the *Bibliography*.
[8] *Ross* (1944), p. 31.
[9] See *Williams* (1963) for one recent example.

Chapter Two

FACETS OF A COMMAND

2.1. Preliminaries. Before development of the formal machinery needed for a systematic exploration of the logical theory of commands can be begun profitably, various key characteristics of commands must be examined and clarified by pressing the analysis of commands as far as possible in an informal way. The present chapter is devoted to such preliminary spadework.

2.2. The Performative 'Giving of a Command' *versus* **'the Command Given'.** The *giving of a command* to someone — like *making an assertion* (statement) to him — is an historical human transaction that takes place in time, and involves a specific and concrete context of person, place, and occasion. The giving of a command is a performance. From this angle, a 'logic of commands' is difficult to envisage. Performances cannot stand in logical relations to one another, and specifically, one performance cannot entail or imply another, nor can the *description* of one performance entail that of another[1]. And this is as true of making

---

[1] This is not to say that one performance cannot entail as precondition the existence of another of a certain type, as, for example, the issuing of a divorce decree presupposes the prior performance of a marriage.

assertions as of giving commands. (From the fact that Smith *said* 'No Tuesdays are sunny days' on some occasions it certainly does not follow that Smith *said* 'No sunny days are Tuesdays' on that occasion, although to be sure the second quoted statement is logically equivalent with the first.) We shall abstract from this performative aspect of command-giving just as the logic of assertion abstracts from the performative aspect of statement-making. Exactly as standard (assertoric) logic occupies itself almost solely with *the content of the assertion* made in a statement (as apart from the personal and historical setting of its assertion)[2], so our logical theory of commands will dwell in the abstract upon the content of *the command given* or *the order issued* (as apart from the particular speech-performance by which it was given and the concrete occasion for its being given). For us, the key element of a command is not a concrete performance but an abstract *meaning-content* that is conveyed when this command is given. The 'logic of commands' that we envisage does not deal with commands as performances, but rather sets itself the task of elucidating the logical relationships between the *instructions* (or directions) conveyed by commands[3].

[2] We say 'almost' with statements like 'It is *now* raining *here*', in mind.

[3] We leave aside exploration of the relationship between commands and such cognate but non-command items as promises or ought-claims (i.e., assertions of duty). A great deal can be said on this head. For example, as is remarked in *Sellars* (1963), p. 169, there is an interesting inverse relationship between promising and commanding with respect to resultant obligations. While X's (properly) promising something to Y creates a corresponding obligation on X's part, X's (properly) commanding something to Y creates a corresponding obligation on Y's part.

2.3. The Source. Every standard command has a *source*: it emanates from some issuing agency; it must be *given by* someone. The source may be either a single individual or a corporate 'individual', i.e., a duly constituted group (e.g., a parliament or board of directors)[4]. The source of a command is, in all standard cases at any rate, a *person* (and indeed an *agent*) in the sense of moral philosophers.

This feature (among others) serves to differentiate commands from moral imperatives and from 'commandments' which not only can but *prima facie* should be regarded as sourceless. ('Keep your promises!' need not — and indeed should not — be regarded as a 'command of God' nor 'of society' nor 'of conscience'. Apart from far-fetched theories regarding the nature of their sanction, moral imperatives fail to be commands precisely because of their lack of a source[5].) Again, an imperative like that of the placard 'Your country needs you: Join the Army today!' is not properly to be regarded as a command, in part because

---

[4] 'It makes no difference whether the source of the command be an actual individual or a collective body . . .' *Sigwart* (1895), p. 17, notes.

[5] This of course is no reason to think that the 'logic' of moral imperatives is different from that of commands. And in fact moral imperatives provide an important bridge linking the logic of commands on the one hand and deontic logic on the other: the deontic proposition 'One ought to do *A*'/'One ought not to do *A*' can — it is held — be construed as an imperative 'Do *A*!'/'Do not do *A*!' with some characteristic sort of exclamation mark. An extensive literature has grown up regarding the possibility of this equation without leading (in my opinion) to any decisive result. See *Bergström* (1962*b*), pp. 52–93, for a substantial discussion and for references to the literature.

it lacks a genuine source, though perhaps also for other reasons as well.

2.4. The Recipient. Every command has a recipient or addressee: it is directed at some target; it must be *given to* someone. The recipient of a command may be either a single individual or the individuals of some group (set of individuals). Often, indeed generally, the recipient of a command is not specified in the formulation of the command locution, but is implicit in and clear from the context. (This of course holds for other elements of the command as well, and specifically for the source[6].)

Strictly speaking, the recipient of a standard command should be a (single or corporate) person or group of persons. To be sure there are rather extended applications: Jesus commanded the waves. To speak of addressing a command to a computing machine (by means of its program) is not to stretch the proprieties past permissible limits — at any rate we shall assume that it is not so in the rather liberal and broad sense of 'commanding' laid down above. One can certainly address commands to animals[7].

It is a reasonable but not unexceptionable general rule that the recipient of a command be distinct from its source. When the vice chancellor of the university issues an order to the deans, then he issues (*qua* vice

---

[6] *Hofstadter and McKinsey* (1939) distinguish between *directives* (imperatives in which the addressee is specified, e.g., 'John, go away!') and *fiats* (where no addressee is specified, e.g.,' Let there be light!'). Unhappily they decide to concentrate upon the logic of the latter, and as a result much of their work is irrelevant or inapplicable to the logical theory of commands.

[7] Compare *Wellman* (1960), pp. 242–243.

chancellor) an order to himself (*qua* dean) when he has assumed the deanship during a period of vacancy. Another example is the 'first-person plural command' of the 'OK, let's go!' or 'Let us pray!' type. Here the source of the command issues (*qua* source) an order to himself (*qua* member of the recipient group) *inter alia*.

In extraordinary cases it becomes necessary not only to discriminate between the *intended* and the *actual* recipient of a command — it being obviously possible to misaddress a command — but one must also recognize that a command may be addressed to what the source believed mistakenly (sc. cautiously believed to be possibly) a genuine target. (The guard shouts, 'Halt, whoever goes there!' at a dimly-perceived moving shape that turns out to be a wind-blown bush; or the supposed addressee is not a qualified recipient — having been drugged, for example.) And as with any sort of *transmission* there is in addition to the possibility of misaddress also the possibility of misunderstanding or misconstruction.

A command can be addressed to a group of recipients, say the individuals of the set X, in at least two importantly distinct ways:

(i) DISTRIBUTIVELY — to each and every individual member of X ('Every one of you chaps raise your right hand!');

(ii) COLLECTIVELY — to an indifferent subgroup of the members of X possibly including the entire lot ('Some of you chaps carry that table over here!').

12

In the first case each member of the group is required to do something, in the second something is to be done by members of the group without any specific indication of who is to do what. Various sorts of situations are tabulated in Table 1.

TABLE 1: SOME EXAMPLES OF COMMANDS WITH VARIOUS TYPES OF SOURCES AND RECIPIENTS

Individual to Individual
John to Tom: Get up!

Individual to Group (*Collective*)
Lieutenant to platoon: Form ranks!

Individual to Group (*Distributive*)
Jesus to Disciples: Go ye into the world . . .!

Group (*Collective*) *to Individual*
Cease and desist order from court to individual

Group (*Collective*) *to Group* (*Collective*)
Court order to a corporation to divest itself of certain corporate holdings (in violation of antitrust statutes)

Group (*Collective*) *to Group* (*Distributive*)
Court order to residents of some area to vacate it for public purposes

Group (*Distributive*) *to Individual*
Crowd to Pilate: Let Barrabas go free!

Group (*Distributive*) *to Group* (*Collective*)
Demonstrators at city council: Lower our taxes!

Group (*Distributive*) *to Group* (*Distributive*)
Demonstrators to group of U.S. visitors: Go home, Yankees!

13

2.5. Chain of Command. Commands are almost invariably couched in the second person (singular or plural). But third person commands are possible, as witness the following:

Mother to Johnny's sister Mary: 'Johnny is to come home now!'

Commanding general to colonel of a regiment: 'The 3rd company is to move along line A starting at 8 a.m. sharp!'

Such commands are in fact orders to *convey* or *transmit* a command: X orders Y to pass some order on to Z. Such command transmission functions generally in the context of an authority structure that may range from a very informal arrangement to a formalized 'chain of command'. In some cases the 'transmission' of the command virtually amounts to mere 'message carrying' (e.g., the Mary–Johnny example) and in other cases the intermediary may lend the (conceivably even indispensable) 'weight of his own authority' to the transmitted order. In general, when X commands Y to order Z to do A we may gloss this as complex consisting of three commands:

1. X orders Z to do A (where X conveys this order to Z via Y).

2. X orders Y to see to it that Z (2a) *receives* and (2b) *carries out* his order.

The extent to which (2b) is operative — i.e., the extent to which the transmitter is authorized to see to it that the recipient executes the command — determines whether the case is merely one of 'message-carrying' or of a genuine 'chain of command'.

14

Facets of a Command

In a recent paper[8], Mark Fisher considers *iterated* commands of the type:

$$X \text{ orders } Y \text{ to order } Z \text{ to do } A$$

Introducing the notation

$$Oxy(A)$$

to mean 'x orders y to do A'— the initial command would thus be rendered as $Oxy(Oyz(A))$ — Fisher considers various possible rules for the logic of this notion. He finds one particular principle to be unproblematically acceptable:

$$Oxy(Oyz(A)) \text{ entails } Oxz(A)$$

But even this plausible principle is not so straightforward a matter as it might seem, since it overlooks the essential need here for a *chain of command*. When this requirement is not met — or when the 'chain' is broken — we obtain the anomaly illustrated in the following example[9]:

Suppose an armed forces scientist of country A, who is a major, is on the enemy payroll, and directs a team of several captains, loyal to country A, who are working on project P under his command. Suppose further that one day our traitorous major gets an order from the enemy embassy: 'Order your captains to stop working on project P.' Has the embassy ordered the captains to stop work on P? Does this even make sense given the absolute loyalty of the captains to country A?

[8] *Fisher* (1961).
[9] Due to Dr E. Sosa.

We shall here make no attempt to treat iterated 'chain of command' commands as a separate category; rather we view them as an especially complex sort of context for commands of the ordinary sort.

2.6. Entitlement, Justification, Inappropriate Commands. Generally speaking, the source should have some *entitlement* or *authority* for giving a command to its recipient — i.e., he occupies some status *vis à vis* the recipient that puts him into a position to exact compliance or at least to elicit co-operation (e.g., he is the recipient's parent or teacher or commanding officer)[10]. Such entitlement may in certain cases be assumed without any status-based backing, as when someone simply 'takes charge' at the scene of an accident or disaster[11]. Moreover, a command generally has some *justification* — i.e., the source should be in a position to provide a rational and reasonable answer to the question of why he issued a certain command[12]. A

[10] Note that it is the mutual relationship that is crucial. When the lieutenant shouts 'Present arms!' on the parade ground, it is the men in *his* company who answer to his command which even the lowliest private of an adjacent company is free, and indeed duty-bound to ignore.

[11] There are borderline cases. Is the passer-by who shouts 'Jump!' at a pedestrian endangered by an oncoming car giving a command? Also, there are gratuitous or unwarranted 'assumptions of authority' to command : ' "I think you ought to go, Dorothea" said Mr Prong; and even Rachel could perceive that there was some slight touch of authority in his voice. It was the slightest possible intonation of a command, but, nevertheless, it struck Rachel's ears'. (A. Trollope, *Rachel Ray*, ch. 20.)

[12] Although a command can patently be justified in this way, it surely cannot be said to *follow* from its justification in the logical sense of the term. Compare *McGuire* (1961).

command can thus be 'questioned' by its recipient both as regards the authority of its source and his grounds for giving it.

It might be in order to develop some taxonomy of inappropriate commands. These would include (perhaps among others): (1) *improper* (or perhaps *impertinent*) commands, which the source is not entitled to give to the recipient (as a private cannot order a general about, nor the general a civilian); (2) *overreaching* commands which require of the recipient more than can reasonably be asked *of him* for example, by asking of him that which is physically impossible *for him* ('Henry, lift that weight!' where it weighs 1000 pounds); (3) and *absurd* commands which can be of two types, either (i) making a requirement which the recipient cannot meet because it is based on a false factual presupposition ('Henry, drive your car to the house!' where Henry has no car), or (ii) making a requirement which *no-one whatsoever* can meet because this is logically or physically impossible ('Henry, divide 2 into 113 without a remainder!').

Our discussion, however, will abstract entirely from this matter of the source's authority or entitlement for commanding the recipient and his warrant or justification for issuing the particular command to him: we shall confine attention to the command itself. Just as in standard logic one deals solely with the content of utterances (or possible utterances) rather than with the speaker's epistemic warrant for the statements he makes, so our 'logic of commands' will occupy itself primarily with the *content* of commands (or possible commands)[13].

2.7. The Mooted Action or Result; Positive *versus* Negative Commands. The pivotal component of a command is its mooted action or result — the possible process of activity or state of affairs which the source enjoins the target to do or achieve or to refrain from doing or achieving. We correspondingly distinguish between *action-performance commands* ('Raise your hands!') and achievement or *state-realization commands* ('Learn French!' or 'Go to sleep!' or 'Go West, young man!'). A performance command orders a certain particular activity or set of activities, while a realization command orders the achievement of a certain state of affairs without — in the 'pure' cases, at any rate — specifying anything whatever as to the set of activities by which this is to be achieved (*'Look*

[13] The distinction between a command and what for want of a better word I shall call an *imprecation* ('Would that ... happen', 'May ... happen', 'Let ... happen') is threefold: (1) an imprecation does not need to have an addressee, and even when it *does* have an addressee, (2) the thing at issue may not be within his power (i.e., we can say 'Would that you, Smith, were 3 inches shorter!' but we cannot command him to bring it about), and (3) the source of an imprecation may not be authorized to give a corresponding command (an employee may properly make the imprecation 'Would that the chief gave us the afternoon off!' but cannot properly command him to do so). When there is an addressee of an imprecation, *and* the asked-for item is in his power, *and* the source is entitled to exact obedience from the addressee, then the line between imprecation and command seems to become a thin one, a matter of stylistic courtesy alone. (Much the same can be said of *requests* of the 'Would you please ...' type.)

about for your glasses!' *versus* '*Find* your glasses!')[14].
A state-realization command typically leaves open to
its addressee a vast range of alternative courses of
action in compliance: 'See to it that the window is
opened!' (he need not even do it himself), 'Make pile
(1) larger than pile (2)!' (he may add to (1) or take
away from (2) or do some combination thereof). (An
action-performance command can of course also be
indefinite as to various modes of compliance-action —
'Raise one hand!' does not indicate which hand is to
be raised, how high to raise it, whether to raise it
swiftly or slowly, etc. This last-named command
illustrates another complexity, because it lies at the
fuzzy border between the action-performance command 'Select one of your hands for raising and raise
it!' and the state-realization command 'Realize the
circumstance that one of your hands is raised up!'.)

We have already committed ourselves to the
principle that the performance of the mooted action
(or the attainment of the mooted result) must be something which it is reasonable to suppose to lie within the

[14] One important 'logical' difference between an action and a
state-realization (achievement) is that the former can be
iterated (resulting in a repetition of the action) whereas the
latter cannot. Thus 'Say "AH" and say "AH"!' is equivalent
with 'Say "AH" twice!' whereas 'Find your pen and find your
pen!' must be construed as either a puzzling redundancy or
an utter nonsense.

The fact that the logic of commands deals at once with both
state-realization and action-performance is a point of contact
with deontic logic of which writers on this latter subject have
been insufficiently aware, usually confining their discussion to
the obligatoriness, permittedness, and forbiddenness (pro-
hibitedness) solely to the performance of acts to the exclusion
of the obtaining of states-of-affairs.

19

addressee's power. This view requires us to regard certain seemingly simple commands as abbreviated substitutes for other more complicated ones. For example, we propose to construe the command:

'Recall your acquaintance's name!'

as short for

'Make every effort to recall your acquaintance's name and keep this up until you do recall it!'

since recall and non-recall do lie outside the region of our voluntary control. Again, if judge X orders the accused Y to undergo a certain punishment, we reconstrue this as a command that Y undergo this punishment — i.e., as an order to the appropriate authorities to inflict this punishment upon Y.

We shall further speak of the positive or negative *quality* of a command according as it orders its recipient to do or to forbear doing. A command is positive when a certain action is ordered ('Open this window!') or the realization of a certain state is enjoined ('Get these people out of this room!'). And a command is negative when a certain action is prohibited by it ('Pray thou not for this people, neither lift up a cry or prayer for them!' *Jeremiah* 11: 14), or the realization of a certain state is forbidden by it ('Learn not the way of the heathen, and be not dismayed at the signs of heaven!' *Jeremiah* 10: 2). In very many cases it is essentially arbitrary whether a command is to be regarded as positive or negative (consider the pair 'Keep your voice down!'— 'Don't raise your voice!'; or the pair [addressed to a standing person] 'Don't sit down!'— 'Keep standing up!').

20

It should be noted that 'mental-action' commands are more often realization-commands than performance-commands ('Remember [i.e., 'keep in mind'] your partner's name!'). Furthermore, action-performance commands and state-realization commands can in some instances approach close to one another ('Look about for the book until you find it!', 'Find the book!').

2.8. Manner-of-execution Specification. A further discriminable component of commands is their *manner-of-execution specification* indicating the mode, method, procedure, means, or other aspects of the *manner* in which the mooted action is to be done (refrained from) or the mooted state-of-affairs realized (prevented). Some examples are: 'Shut the window *slowly and carefully*!', 'Shut the window *by pressing it downwards gently*!', 'Shut the window *with the window-pole*!' This manner-of-execution specification is often tacit rather than explicitly specified.

2.9. Execution-timing. An important characteristic of any command revolves about its execution-timing.

Here we must distinguish between:

(i) *Do-it-now commands*. Certain commands require that something be done (or realized) at once. For example: 'Close the window!'

(ii) *Do-it-always commands* or *standing orders*. Certain commands require that something be 'done' constantly and always, strange though this may seem because it is rather strained to speak of *doing* here. For example: 'Don't

c   21

inflict needless pain!!', 'Keep to the path of righteousness!!'[15]

We shall adhere to the convention that to emphasize that a certain command is a standing order (do-it-always command) we affix a pair of exclamation marks. Thus 'Act prudently!' could be taken as 'Act prudently *now*!' but 'Act prudently!!' can only be construed as 'Act prudently *always*!'

Of course the 'now' of a do-it-now command must not be taken too seriously. It does not necessarily mean '*instanter* and in the twinkling of an eye'[16] but rather something like 'within a reasonable and appropriate interval'[17]. Thus 'Read every book on the shelf!' is a 'do-it-now' command in our semi-technical sense of the term.

---

[15] These two are our basic paradigms. There are certainly other possibilities, such as commands which give the recipient discretion in execution-timing (see, e.g., section 4 of Chapter Four) but these can be accommodated within the present framework by suitable expedients.

[16] Or, 'in about half no time', as the Queen of Hearts puts it in *Alice in Wonderland*.

[17] We shall abstract entirely from certain difficulties regarding 'now' statements. For example, '*X* is now driving from Los Angeles to New York' is perfectly compatible with '*X* is now driving towards Los Angeles and away from New York', if the first 'now' envisages a long-term period and the second a short-term period (say because following a sinuous mountain road requires such a reversal for a short while). (I owe this example to John Robison.) Complications of this sort have no special bearing on the logic of commands — they arise in assertoric tense logic, and we shall simply assume here that they can be settled there in a way adequate to the needs of the inquiry we have in hand.

Another aspect of execution-timing that may be present in certain commands is the execution-deadline. This gives rise to 'do-it-then' and 'do-it-by-then' commands. Examples: 'Get all the furniture out of this room by noon tomorrow!', 'Memorize these data before our next class meeting!', 'Open this window at 3 p.m. tomorrow!' We shall, however, treat all such commands not as a special type unto themselves, but as conditional commands of a certain sort. (See section 4.4 below.)

2.10. Execution-precondition. Another important component or possible component of a command is the setting of conditions specifying the occasions for its execution.

Here we shall distinguish primarily between

(i) *One-shot conditional commands* or *when-next commands*. These have the type-paradigm 'The next time that such and such a condition is satisfied, do so-and-so!' We have such examples as: 'When Henry returns, tell him I've gone out!' and 'When the postman comes, give him this letter!'

(ii) *Conditional standing orders (commands)* or *whenever-commands*. These have the paradigm: 'Whenever such and such a condition is satisfied, do so-and-so!!' We have such examples as: 'When it's rainy, carry an umbrella!!', 'When you drive grandmother about, go slowly!!' and even 'Brush your teeth every morning!!' (i.e., 'Wherever a new morning is at hand, brush your teeth!!').

23

Commands which would, on the ordinary view of things, be taken as operative for the future (such as 'Unlock this door at noon tomorrow!') can — and for our subsequent purposes will — be construed as one-shot conditional commands with a temporal condition ('When noon arrives tomorrow, unlock this door!'). On this approach, a do-it-now command becomes a one-shot conditional command with a 'when the time is now' condition. Analogously, a do-it-always command can be viewed as a standing conditional command with a trivial or empty condition. And a 'do-it-during-a-certain-period command' can be regarded as a do-it-always command of a special sort ('Write me every Wednesday this October!' $\cong$ 'Write me whenever it is a Wednesday of this October!!'[18]). These remarks will be put to work in our subsequent formal analysis.

When a command is conditional, its condition may be either overt or explicit on the one hand ('When it rains, close the windows!!') or tacit or implicit on the other ('Drive carefully!!' $\cong$ 'When you drive, drive carefully!!'). When no conditions are involved, the command may be said to be *peremptory* or *categorical* ('Close that window!').

Even a peremptory command could be construed as involving tacit conditions of an 'other things being equal' sort. The line of demarcation between peremptory and implicitly conditional commands is in any event a fuzzy one. A case could be made out, for example, for regarding 'If you live to do' as a condition

---

[18] We use the symbol '$\cong$' to stand between different verbal or symbolic formulations of 'the same command'.

24

implicitly present in every command (and possibly other, equally obvious, tacit conditions as well). Thus 'Shut the window!' ≅ 'Shut the window now, *if you live to do so*!'[19] and 'Always remember the 5th of November!!' ≅ 'Always remember the 5th of November *so long as you live*!!'. On the other hand, some *prima facie* conditional commands are peremptory. '*X*, never hit a man when he's down!!' ≅ '*X*, hitting a man who is down — that's always out!!'

A conditional command may be called *inoperative* so long as and whenever its condition is not realized, and correspondingly be said to become *operative* when its condition is realized.

2.11. Period for Being in Force. Any (actually given) command will be in force for some period of time after it is given. It can lapse from being in force in one of two ways, namely (1) by being cancelled (annulled, withdrawn, countermanded), or (2) by lapsing or becoming 'chronologically inoperative' as with 'Smith, the next time *X* happens, do *Y*!' or 'Smith, always do *Y* until the next time that *X* happens!' after *X* has (next) happened. Military orders often specify their in-force period explicitly, as in the following example:

1. All personnel in the company are to do *XYZ* daily.

2. This order is to become effective on . . . (date) and will remain in effect for a period of thirty days.

---

[19] Or 'if it isn't smashed by a falling meteorite', or the like. Even in a categorical command a *ceteris paribus* 'condition' should always be understood as tacitly present.

It should be noted, however, that a pre-fixedly terminating command of the type 'Do *X* every day! is to be in force until *D*-date' may be construed as equivalent with the explicitly conditional command 'On every day prior to and including *D*-date, do *X*!'

2.12. 'Inter Alia' Rider. A command of the type '*X*, do *A* when *P*!' is to be construed as having a tacit *inter alia* rider. It must not be read as saying to 'do *A* only' but as saying to 'do *A inter alia*'. The command 'Smith, write Aunt Jane every other day!' would be over-fulfilled (as it were) if Smith writes her every day — unlike the command 'Smith, write Aunt Jane *only* every other day!', which would then be disobeyed. Thus the command '*X*, do *A* when *P*!' and '*X*, do *B* when *P*!' (given by the same source to the same recipient on the same occasion) must be taken to supplement and not to cancel one another wherever *A* and *B* are compatible. And if *Y* commands *X* to 'Do *A* and *B*!', then *Y* is entitled to claim 'I have commanded *X* to do *A*'— without admitting to any change of mind, and without having to regard the second command as a new one, rather than as a partial restatement of the old one.

Chapter Three

TERMINOLOGY AND SYMBOLISM

3.1. The Command Requirement. The notion of a *command requirement* is introduced to serve as systematic counterpart to the informal idea of 'what accomplishments a command requires', considered apart from such things as who it is that gives the command, to whom it is given, under what conditions it becomes operative, and the like. Specifically, a command requirement is to comprise the following items:

(i) the mooted action or result

(ii) the manner-of-execution specification

(iii) the positive or negative quality of the command.

Some examples of command requirements are:

(a) opening the window carefully with the window-pole

(b) finding Smith's lost dog

(c) refraining from irritating Aunt Jane

27

(d) carrying out emergency procedure number 32 to the very letter

(e) carrying through to completion an edition of the *Opera Omnia* of Archimedes

(f) recalling the name of one's favourite old school chum.

The command requirement corresponds to the idea of 'what it is that the command instructs its recipient to do or avoid doing (when once it becomes operative in the case of a conditional command)'.

A (pure) *command* — in the technical sense of the *content* of a command or 'the command given'— is a composite specification of:

(i) the command requirement

(ii) the command execution precondition, if there is to be one

(iii) the character of the command as either one-shot ('when-next') or standing ('whenever').

The actual 'giving' of a command involves the composite specification of the pure command itself together with a source and a recipient, and an occasion — and thus a time t_0 — at which this command is given to this recipient. The performatory giving of a command thus involves, in addition to the command itself three further factors: (i) a *source* who gives this command to (ii) the *recipient* in (iii) some specific *circumstance* or on some specific *occasion*. Our interest being focused upon the commands themselves, these *performatory characteristics* of (an actually given) command concern us here in only an incidental way,

28

i.e., only insofar as they bear upon an analysis of 'the command given' itself. (Note the locutions 'He gave the same command to another chap an hour ago', and 'Another chap gave him the same command an hour ago', where the giving-performances are obviously different, though the commands themselves are clearly thought of as being one and the same.)

3.2. What can Serve as a Command Requirement?
What sorts of things can appropriately be required by a command? This question can best be answered in terms of an analysis of the functions served by commands. Putting the matter as briefly as possible — and thus somewhat dogmatically — a command is given:

- (i) to effect action, and specifically to induce its recipient to the course of action that constitutes *compliance* with the command
- (ii) to do this by serving not as a *cause*, but as a *reason* for action, inducing its recipient to a deliberate, intentional response.

This being so, the only things which a command can appropriately require are those actions or courses of action that lie within the area of conscious human control. *A command must be realizable,* where 'to realize a requirement' essentially means 'to bring it about (deliberately or intentionally) that what the requirement requires in fact obtains'. Thus any possible human doing, i.e., anything which 'lies within the power of' men to do or not to do, can serve as a command requirement. Anything impossible — logically, physically, or conceptually (e.g., altering the past) — has to be excluded. (The determination of such impossibility is of course always a matter of assertoric logic and is thus not a special problem for the logic of commands.) Nor can a command require that something be done inadvertently or accidentally or unwittingly, etc.

This view of the matter requires us to put a conforming gloss upon certain commands which *prima facie* appear to require matters beyond our control. For example, since recollection is not a thing over which we exercise deliberate control, the command 'Recall the name of your first teacher!' should — on the present view — be construed as '*Make every effort* to remember the name of your first teacher and *keep this up* until you succeed in recalling it!' Similarly the command 'Salute officers automatically and out of habit!' should be construed as '*Take the measures required* to form the habit of saluting officers automatically and *keep this up* until you get the habit!'

3.3. Notation for a Formal Analysis of Commands. We shall adopt some special abbreviative notations:

$t, t', t_0, t_1, t_2, t_3, \ldots$ to represent *times*, i.e., dates or specific periods of time.

$X, Y, Z, X_1, Y_2, Z_3, \ldots$ to represent *command addressees* (non-empty sets of agents).

$A, B, C, A_1, B_2, C_3, \ldots$ to represent possible *command requirements*, that is, actions or courses of action leading to mooted results.

Formally speaking, these will be propositional functions of two variables (parameters), an agent X and a time t, such that '$A(X,t)$' becomes a statement to the effect that 'X does A at t'[1] or perhaps 'X realizes A at t'. Such requirements can be regarded as subject to modification by the use of logical connectives. In particular, given two command requirements A and B, we define:

  i. $\sim A$ as the command requirement that is satisfied when A is not done (is refrained from, is not brought about, etc.).

 ii. $A \& B$ as the command requirement that is satisfied when both A and B are done (carried out, brought about, etc.)[2].

P, Q, R, P_1, Q_2, R_3, ... to represent *command execution preconditions*, i.e., propositional functions of one variable (parameter), a time t, such that '$P(t)$' becomes a statement to the effect that 'P obtains at time t'.

* * *

We can now introduce the following symbolic conventions:

[X ! $A/(P)$] is to mean 'X, the next time (or "at the next juncture at which" or "on the next occasion on which") P obtains, *you are to realize A!*' or equivalently: 'X, if t_0 is the next time t at which $P(t)$ obtains, then you are to bring it about that X-realizes-A-at-t_0 (i.e., that $A(X, t_0)$)!'.

[X ! A/P] is to mean 'X, anytime (or "at any juncture

---

[1] Note that A and t must be compatible. If A is 'writing Aunt Jane every day', then t can be a period of a week, but not a minute or an hour.

[2] For these conceptions and their cognates see *von Wright* (1963), especially Chapter III on 'Act and Ability' and IV on 'The Logic of Action'.

at which" or "on every occasion on which") *P* obtains, you are to realize *A*!' or equivalently: '*X*, at any (non-past) time *t* at which *P(t)* obtains, you are to bring it about that *X*-realizes-*A*-at-*t* (i.e., that *A(X, t)*)!'[3].

This symbolism captures our two command paradigms: (conditional) when-next commands and (conditional) standing orders.

Given the foregoing abbreviative conventions we have that

[Smith! not telling Jones where Robinson is/ (Jones comes here)]

abbreviates

'Smith, don't tell Jones where Robinson is when Jones (next) comes here!'

and

[Tom! speaking loudly and clearly/Tom speaks to Bob]

abbreviates

'Tom, speak loudly and clearly whenever you speak to Bob!!'[4]

---

[3] This definition, as well as the preceding, abstracts from the fact that it would be normal to admit of some short interval or 'period of grace' between the time realization of the condition *P* and the realization of the requirement *A*. It can (and perhaps should) be so construed throughout the ensuing discussion.

[4] Sometimes a *prima facie* simple command is in fact complex. Thus 'Tom and Bob, help each other move that table!' does *not* amount to the unitary command [{Tom, Bob}! helping each other move that table/now] but to the pair of commands: [Tom! helping Bob move that table/now] and [Bob! helping Tom move that table/now]. The *prima facie* simple requirement has to be split apart into two distinct ones. (Note that braces occur here in their common use for set-formation.)

Somewhat less obviously

> [Jim! helping Bob as much as he needs to be helped insofar as you are able to do so/Bob needs help]

would render

'Jim, give Bob all the help you can!!'

One can, and we shall, take only $[X \mathbin{!} A/P]$ as primitive, defining $[X \mathbin{!} A/(P)]$ as $[X \mathbin{!} A/P^{\#}]$ where $P^{\#}$ is the precondition not simply 'that P obtains', but 'that it is the *next occasion on which* P obtains'. Thus if t_0 is the time at which the command is given, then $P^{\#}$ may be defined as follows:

$$P^{\#}(t) \;=\; Df\, P(t) \;\&\; \sim (\exists\, t')\, [(t_0 \leqslant t' < t) \;\&\; P(t')]$$

Other complex commands could also be defined. For example, the command 'X, do A until B occurs!' considered as being given at time t_0, may be construed as the command $[X \mathbin{!} \text{doing } A/B^+]$ where

$$B^+(t) \;=\; \sim B(t) \;\&\; \sim (\exists\, t')\, [(t_0 \leqslant t' < t) \;\&\; B(t')]$$

Again, the command 'X do A only if B occurs!' $\cong$ $[X \mathbin{!} \text{refraining from doing } A/B \text{ does not occur}]$.

* * *

In rendering one and the same command by this symbolic machinery, alternative formulations may be possible. Consider, for example, the command

'X, plant corn three days after the next rainfall!'

which could, with equal appropriateness, be rendered either as

(a) [*X*! planting corn after an interval of three days/(It is a rainy day)]

or, alternatively, as

(b) [*X*! planting corn/(It is the third day after a rainy day)]

We shall adopt the course of having the command requirement be free (i.e., as free as possible) from any temporal reference, and therefore regard (b) — in contrast to (a) — as the standard rendition of this command.

It should thus be noted that commands as we conceive of them involve a *timeless* requirement, together with an execution-condition stipulating that this requirement be met at certain times (either 'now' or in certain 'future' cases, or both), the temporal origin or reference-point being fixed by the time-of-giving of the command. Several authors[5] have hoped to see the logic of imperatives developed in strict parallel with the assertoric (indicative) logic of tensed statements. (Indeed, for R. M. Hare, the tenseless character of commands is a contingent and remediable feature, and he thinks it proper to 'assume that a logician is entitled to construct imperatives in all persons and in all tenses'.) Our view of commands rejects this conception, taking them to be inescapably oriented towards the present and/or future[6].

---

[5] For example, see *Hare* (1949) and *Hare* (1952), pp. 187–188.
[6] Compare *Wellman* (1961), p. 243.

Thus the argument

> Do *A* whenever *P* is the case!!
> P will be the case tomorrow
> ———————————————
> Do *A* tomorrow!

would seem (to anticipate later matters) a plausible mode of command inference. But it is clear that the closely similar argument

> Do *A* whenever *P* is the case!!
> P was the case yesterday
> ———————————————
> Do *A* yesterday!

is highly implausible: indeed wholly unacceptable. The command 'Do *A* whenever *P* is the case!!' should be construed as '*Now and henceforward:* Do *A* whenever *P* is the case!!'

*　　*　　*

Another convention will be adopted. When a command actually has no execution precondition, being a peremptory or categorical command, we shall treat it as a conditional command with a vacuous (empty, trivial) condition — say 'The sun is either shining or not'. We represent this vacuous condition by *. Thus

[Jones! closing that door/(*)]

represents the one-shot peremptory command

> Jones, close that door (now)!

and

[Tom! being prudent/*]

represents the peremptory standing order

> Tom, be prudent (always)!!

35

Consider the command, '*X*, whenever you meet friends, greet all of them!!' This can be represented by:

[*X*! greeting all the friends *X* meets/*X* meets friends]

But it is clear that this also amounts simply to:

[*X*! greeting all the friends *X* meets/*]

The command [*X*! *A*/*P*] can be regarded as equivalent with [*X*! *A*/*] whenever *A* is such that the satisfaction of the precondition *P* is automatically built into its formulation.

It is important to stress that — as things are being set up here — a command [*X*! *A*/*P*] will not be well-formed when *A* and *P* have any free variables other than a temporal parameter (*t*, *t'*, etc.). Thus the commands

(1) *X*, whenever you meet a friend, greet him!!

(2) Keep all your promises!!

(3) *X*, whenever anyone gives you something, thank him for it!!

(4) Say 'please' to anyone when asking him for anything!!

cannot be represented as:

(1a) [*X*! greeting *x*/you meet *x* and *x* is a friend of yours]

(2a) [— !*f*/you have promised to do *f*][7]

---

[7] A dash shall be used to represent the second person singular, so that [— ! *A*/*P*] = *You* are to do *A* whenever *P*!!

36

(3a) [*X*! thanking *x* for *u*/*x* has given *u* to *X*]

(4a) [— ! saying 'please' to *x*/you ask *x* for something]

Instead, the four initial commands must be represented in our notation as:

(1b) [*X*! greeting every friend you meet/*]

(2b) [— ! keeping all your promises/*]

(3b) [*X*! thanking everyone who gives you something for giving it to you/*]

(4b) [— ! saying 'please' (then and there) to everyone you ask for anything/*]

We shall also introduce some symbolism to make explicit the *mode of address* of the command recipient, in the event that the recipient is a group. We shall write:

(i) *X* (simply) if the recipient is either an individual or a group being addressed *distributively*

(ii) (*X*) if the recipient is a group being addressed *collectively*.

For present purposes *we shall take the distributive mode of address as our standard case*, and will confine our explicit attention almost exclusively to this case. No difficulties of principle arise in extending the discussion to collectively addressed commands. By this convention, if *X* and *Y* are individuals (unit classes), the inference

$$[\{X, Y\}! A/P]$$
$$\overline{[X! A/P]}$$

is automatically valid, but not the inference to the same conclusion from the premiss:

$$[(\{X, Y\})! A/P]$$

3.4. Alternative Machinery? Several writers have sought to base the theory of commands upon a propositional operator of essentially the following kind:

$$X! p$$

is to mean 'X, bring it about [or *ensure* or *make it true*] that p![8]. This way of analysing commands may be termed the *propositional operator approach*[9].

This approach, however, is impotent to provide a representation for the conditional (or: 'hypothetical') command 'X, do p if (i.e., *upon condition that*) q!. For, symbolizing this last-named command by

$$(1) \quad X! p/q$$

it is not difficult to see that this cannot be represented by the unconditional command operator. The closest we can come is

$$(2) \quad X! (p \text{ if } q)$$

---

[8] Generally some admissibility restriction is placed upon propositions that may be put into this context. (E.g., *Menger* (1939) requires they be neither necessary nor impossible.)

[9] This entire approach derives from *Mally* (1926) and is taken over from this pioneering work (sometimes without acknowledgment) by most subsequent writers who view a 'logic' of commands with favour. See the discussion of *Bergström* (1962*b*), pp. 16–20, who, however, carries 'the operator analysis' back only to *Hofstadter and McKinsey* (1939).

But the non-identity of these commands is readily shown by a consideration of their satisfaction. For X can satisfy (2) by seeing to it that q is not the case, in which case command (2) asks nothing further of him. On the other hand, X's bringing it about that $\sim q$ is not a way of satisfying (1). Furthermore let it be that q is not the case (i.e., is false), and that this is so for reasons wholly outside X's control. In this circumstance, (1) *asks nothing* of X but (2) does ask something of him (viz. that he bring about a certain relationship between p and q).

This would suggest that one should at the least take (1) as the basic, defining '$X ! p$' by the definition:

$$'X ! p' = Df\, 'X ! p/*'$$

where '*' represents some vacuous (inevitably satisfied) condition such as 'the sun is shining or it is not'.

Writers who base a theory of commands upon a propositional command-operator have been oblivious to the impossibility of introducing genuinely conditional commands. Thus, for example, Bergström[10] vacillates between rendering 'X, if p is the case, do q!' one or another of the pair:

(i) If p then: $X ! q$

(ii) $X !$ (If p then q)

He says that 'Natural language is not sufficiently exact on this point'. But in fact the failing lies not so much in the inexactness of natural language as in the

[10] See p. 39 of *Bergström* (1962*b*).

impotence of an (unconditional) propositional command operator to render strictly conditional commands of the 'Do q on condition that p!' type: version (i) is what is wanted, but version (ii) is as close as we can get[11].

Moreover, it must be realized that even the added introduction of such a conditionalized propositional operator will not suffice for our purposes. For let P_1 and P_2 be propositional functions of a single temporal parameter, and consider the command:

X, bring it about that $P_2(t)$ whenever $P_1(t)$![12]

which would be symbolized by the notation given above as

$$[X \text{ ! realizing } P_2/P_1]$$

A fuller (but nonstandard) formulation is:

$$[X \text{ ! realizing } P_2 \text{ at } t/P_1 \text{ at } t], \text{ for all } t$$

This cannot be formulated within the resources of the propositional operator notation, because of the internal presence of a propositional function (of a temporal parameter) rather than a proposition.

It thus appears that in order to deal adequately with the sorts of commands at which our theory is directed, it is necessary to use machinery of the sort introduced in section 3.3, above, which is designed explicitly to

[11] Actually the vacillation between (i) and (ii) goes back to *Mally* (1926), who solves the problem of having to make a choice by the simple expedient of taking '$p \supset !\, q$' and '$!\, (p \supset q)$' as logical equivalents (see pp. 17, 27). The vacillation is sufficiently prominent in the literature to deserve a label — I propose *Mally's Perplex*.

[12] Or perhaps preferably: X, bring it about that $P_2\ (t + \Delta)$ whenever $P_1(t)$!

accommodate temporal considerations. A straightforwardly propositional command operator — be it absolute or even conditional — fails to provide a sufficiently powerful basis for an adequate logical theory of commands.

3.5. Assertoric Reducibility: The Threat Theory.
Certain writers have suggested that the command

$$X, \text{do } A \: ! \cong [X \: ! \: A/(*)]$$

is to be construed as equivalent with

$$\sim (X \text{ does } A) \supset S$$

or equivalently (construing the implication at issue as *material* implication)

$$X \text{ does } A \text{ v } S$$

where 'S' denotes a sanction, i.e., something bad or some undesirable consequence[13]. A command becomes a disjunctive assertion of the form of a threat: Either conform in action or 'take the consequences'. Among the more objectionable — i.e., counterintuitive — consequences of this particular proposal for the construal of commands are the following:

(1) It renders commands as assertoric statements, and thus as straightforward truths and falsehoods.

[13] This approach was first proposed in *Menger* (1939) — see pp. 59–60 — and was adopted (without recognition of Menger's priority) and developed by *Bohnert* (1945). It was adapted to deontic logic and extensively developed by Alan Ross Anderson, *The Formal Analysis of Normative Systems* (New Haven, 1956), and in subsequent papers.

(2) It licenses the inference from 'X does A' to 'X, do A!'

(3) It has the consequence that, for any A, we must have either 'X, do A!' or 'X, do not do A!'

In the face of these considerations, and various others which could be adduced[14], we shall not here adopt the 'threat theory' of commands. It is undoubtedly true that failure to obey an appropriately given command will in general result in a sanction, but it is a far cry from this truism to an analysis of the *meaning* of a command. We shall here treat commands as *sui generis*, without attempting to reconstrue them as assertions of any kind. This topic will be resumed from another angle in Chapter Seven below in considering whether commands can be true or false.

[14] See *Bergström* (1962*b*), pp. 13–15.

Chapter Four

THE REPRESENTATION OF COMMANDS BY 'PROGRAMS'

4.1. Prefatory Remarks. The literature of the logic of commands has generally focused upon certain extremely simple types of commands of the 'performing-an-action-here-and-now' type, based on such paradigms as '*X*, shut the window!' or '*X*, go to *Y*'s house!' This abstraction from the complexity of realistic commands — even such modestly complex cases as '*X*, shut the window whenever it rains!' or '*X*, go to *Y*'s house the next time he asks you to do so!' — tends to trivialize the entire discussion through oversimplification. In view of this, I should like in this chapter to present a bit of machinery adapted from a field where really complicated commands are treated, viz. computer programming — a domain in which relatively few philosophers and theoretical logicians are at home. Adaptation of this machinery of computer instruction-sequences affords a useful device not only for presenting examples of complex commands, but also for examining the implication relationships among command groups, and the like. The essential points will be developed primarily by means of examples.

4.2. Command 'Programs'. We shall suppose that time is discretized into units. The basic unit will be called the '*u*' which may be thought of as a day (year, microsecond). Given this convention, one can construct what we shall call the *discrete representation* of a command by means of a 'program' in a manner now to be explained. The when-next command

'*X*, realize *A* the next time *P* obtains!' $\cong$ [*X* ! *A*/(*P*)]

may be 'programmed' by the following 'flow-diagram':

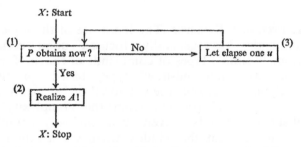

This 'program' is composed of three types of 'boxes' (duly connected by arrows):

   (i) A 'yes-no-question' box ending with a question-mark, viz. (1).

  (ii) A 'letting-time-elapse' or 'time-co-ordinating' box beginning with 'let', viz. (3).

 (iii) An 'instruction-execution' box ending with an exclamation-mark, viz. (2).

The command is a 'terminating' command because it can eventuate in a STOP. An example of a non-terminating command is the whenever command:

'*X*, realize *A* whenever *P* obtains!!' $\cong$ [*X* ! *A*/*P*]

44

this command corresponds to the program:

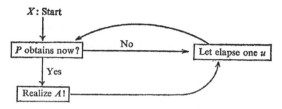

Note that there is an important difference between the *conjunctive* 'and' of 'Do *A* and *B*!' or diagrammatically

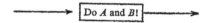

and on the *sequential* 'and' of 'Do *A* and *then* do *B*!' or diagrammatically

There is, however, no difference between

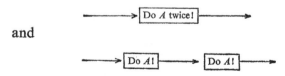

and

The command

'*X*, always realize *A* until *P* occurs!' $\cong$ [*X* ! *A*/*P* has not yet occurred]

45

corresponds to the flow-diagram:

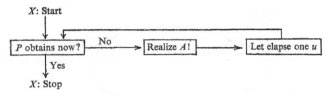

Similarly, the command

'X, always realize A once P has occurred!' $\cong$ [X !
A/P has already occurred]

corresponds to the flow-diagram:

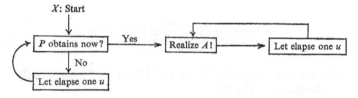

Again, the command 'X, whenever you do A, do B three days later!' can be presented by the program with the following flow-diagram:

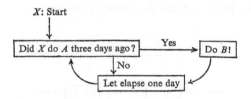

Finally, 'X, do A whenever (but only when) you do B!' corresponds to the flow-diagram[1]:

[1] Note that this flow diagram is — as it should be — substantially unaffected by an interchange of 'A' and 'B'.

46

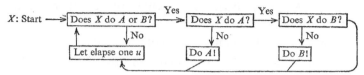

The machinery of command representation can of course also be used to render groups of (appropriately interrelated) commands, i.e., '*sets* of orders (or instructions)'. Thus the pair

Do $A! \cong [- ! A/(*)]$

Do B after the next occasion on which you do $A! \cong [- ! B/(\text{you do } A)]$

can be rendered as simply

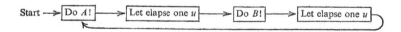

An interesting situation is afforded by what von Wright calls a family of *Sisyphus-orders*[2], which are such that compliance with some of the orders creates a situation in which further orders must inevitably be complied with. An example is that of the command-set

Do A!

Whenever you do A follow it by doing B!!

Whenever you do B follow it by doing A!!

which has the program:

Start →[Do A!]——→[Let elapse one u]——→[Do B!]——→[Let elapse one u]

---

[2] *Von Wright* (1963), p. 147.

The Representation of Commands by 'Programs'

Von Wright's own, somewhat more interesting, illustration is

Whenever the window is open, close it!!

Whenever the window is closed, open it!!

which has the program:

```
Start ──▶│Is the window now open?│──Yes──▶│Close the window!│
                    │No                              ▲
                    ▼                                │
          │Open the window!│──────────▶│Let elapse one u│
```

4.3. Further Examples. Consider the command

$C_1 = $ 'X, do A and B on alternate days, beginning with A today!'

taken as being given on day t_0. This complex command amounts to the two commands

(1) [X ! doing A/It is n days past t_0, with n either 0 or even].

(2) [X ! doing B/It is n days past t_0, with n odd].

This command-complex can be represented by the program[3]:

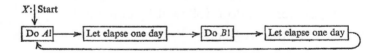

```
X:│Start
   ▼
│Do A!│──▶│Let elapse one day│──▶│Do B!│──▶│Let elapse one day│─┐
   ▲                                                             │
   └─────────────────────────────────────────────────────────────┘
```

[3] Note that this flow diagram has two 'instruction-execution' boxes. It is a theorem which we shall not attempt to prove that when a flow diagram has n such boxes, it can be represented by n commands in our 'normal form' [X ! A/P].

The Representation of Commands by 'Programs'

Compare the command

$C_2 = $ '*X*, do *A* on alternate days, beginning today!'

which amounts to only command (1) above, and is represented by the program:

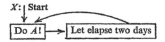

It is clear (a) from the sense of C_1 and C_2, and (b) from their flow-diagrams, that C_1 in a certain sense *entails* C_2. For 'having followed out the flow diagram' of C_1 is something which, in the very nature of things, cannot be done without thereby 'having followed out the flow diagram' of C_2. It is the sense of 'entailment' here at issue that we shall try to capture in our subsequent discussion of the validity of command inferences.

A complex command-instruction can generally be rendered more explicit by some suitably intricate manipulative device. Thus the command 'Thank anyone who gives you a gift!!' $\cong$ [— ! thanking everyone who gives you a gift/*] would correspond to the discrete-representation program:

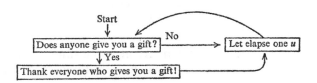

Here the box we have simply given as 'Thank everyone who gives you a gift (now)!' could be represented by some more complex instruction-set such as:

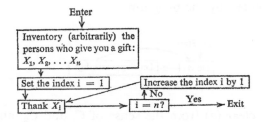

For our present purposes the possibility of such programatic elaborations of internally complex command instructions will simply be ignored: the matter is (from our angle) an unnecessary complication.

4.4. A Complex Case. Special difficulties arise in the presentation by this machinery of commands which allow the addressee discretion in the timing of his compliance-actions. An example would be a command *to X* to do a certain thing *A* (or realize a certain state) at some time or other (i.e., any time of his own choosing during a certain period). (For example, to perform a pilgrimage sometime during his life or to report a change of his address to the authorities within four weeks.) Here we need to introduce an additional new item of notation:

'[*X* ! *A*/{*P*}]' is to mean '*X*, at some time or other (at your discretion) when *P* obtains, you are to realize *A*!'

50

The Representation of Commands by 'Programs'

This command can perhaps be glossed as the unorthodox when-next command $[X \mathbin{!} A_1/(P_1)]$, where

P_1 is 'X's last opportunity to do A when P is at hand'

A_1 is 'not letting it be that X has never done A when P'

The treatment of such commands within the framework of our machinery must in any case be an unorthodox one because the element of *choice* inheres in the discretionary feature of these commands and generates characteristic difficulties. We should have to represent this with something like the following expedient:

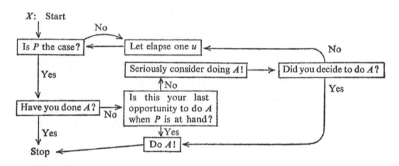

Chapter Five

THE CONCEPT OF COMMAND TERMINATION

5.1. Command Termination. If a command

$$C = [X \mathbin{!} A/P]$$

is considered to be given at some time t, one can form the corresponding (purely assertoric) *command termination statement*:

'$T_t(C)$' for 'X *has (always) realized* A *whenever* P *obtained after time* t'.

For example, if the following command C is supposed to be given at time t,

[Tom! telling Jim to see me/(Tom sees Jim)] $\cong$ 'Tom, tell Jim to see me when (next) you see him!'

The corresponding $T_t(C)$ is,

'Tom did tell Jim to see me when next (after t) he saw him'

52

And if *C* is the command (supposed to be given at *t*),

> [Smith! driving carefully/Smith drives Jones about]
> ≅ 'Smith, drive carefully whenever you drive Jones about!!'

then $T_t(C)$ is,

> 'Smith has driven carefully whenever (after *t*) he drove Jones about'.

The step in linguistic formulation from *C* to $T_t(C)$ is not always a matter of simple, automatic routine. Thus if *C* is 'Roberts, pick up *any one* of these books!' then $T_t(C)$ is not 'Roberts did pick up *any one* of these books (at or shortly after time *t*)', but rather 'Roberts did pick up *some one* of these books'.

Given a command *C*, we shall say that this command is *terminated* as of time *t* whenever $T_t(C)$ is true. A conditional command whose execution precondition never arises will be regarded as automatically terminated (in a trivial way, if you please). Also, we shall say that 'a person *terminates* a command' (as of *t*) when his behaviour is such as to render the appropriate termination statement true. (Note that a standing order only becomes terminated posthumously.) While commands themselves are *prospective* and *ante eventum*, their termination statements are always *retrospective* and *post eventum*.

5.2. Termination and Obedience. It is important to remark that *the truth of* $T_t(C)$ *is a necessary but not sufficient condition for obedience* of the command *C* given at *t*. For consider the following:

(i) Suppose *X* commands *Y* to do *A*, and suppose further that *Y* does do *A* (in the appropriate way). It need not at all be that *Y* has obeyed the command. For example, he might not even have been aware that this specific command was given and have done what the command requires fortuitously. For (genuine[1]) obedience it is clearly requisite that the appropriate action was taken *in response to* the giving of a command. A command is not *strictu sensu* 'obeyed' unless its being given him constitutes for the recipient one of the reasons for his act of compliance.

(ii) But not only must it be 'in response to'— the response must be *of the right kind*. Suppose X commands Y to write his *brother*. Y mishears X, and thinks that he was ordered to write to his *broker*. He does so. But it so happens that his brother *is* his broker. He not only responded to the command, but also did *what* the command required without, however, acting *in the way* the command required. He cannot, I submit, be said — in strict correctness — to have obeyed the command: we will not settle for unintentional compliance when obedience is at issue.

It is therefore correct, proper, and indeed important to distinguish between the termination of a command (i.e., accomplishing what the command asks) on the one hand, and obedience of or compliance with the command (i.e., responding to the command in the requisite way) upon the other. (This distinction could be regarded as an analogue of Kant's distinction

---

[1] It is, of course, possible to say something like: 'I "obeyed" his command without being aware it had been given.' But the sense of 'obedience' here at issue is clearly an extended or figurative one.

between *acting as duty requires* and *acting because duty requires*.)

Correspondingly, it would be appropriate to distinguish between (a) *disobedience* of a command, that is, its intentional nontermination (which, in the case of a conditional command, can occur only if that command becomes operative through realization of its command precondition[2]), and (b) *non-obedience* of a command which occurs when it is neither obeyed nor disobeyed (and which is possible even when the command is successfully terminated).

Termination is a much simpler and less problematic concept than obedience, with respect to which awkward puzzle cases can readily arise. For example: X commands Y to do A, and Y intends to comply, but in the event does A unthinkingly (say from whim or from habit). Did Y *obey* X's command? Again: X commands Y to do A at some future time t_1. Y writes himself a reminder 'Do A at t_1' and when the time comes acts on this reminder, but has by then wholly forgotten X's order and thinks of the reminder-notice as recording a past resolution of his own. Did Y obey X's command? The matter of command obedience is shot through with considerations relating to knowledge and intention from which the matter of command termination is altogether free.

The perspective of command termination is a good one from which to take a retrospective glance at the matter of rational control over commanded actions (cf. section 2 of Chapter Three). The two commands

---

[2] Thus the man who tries genuinely but unsuccessfully to terminate a command does not *disobey* the command, according to our proposed usage.

(1) X, never do A (at all)!!

(2) X, never do A deliberately!!

have the very different termination statements (with respect to t)

($T1$) X never did A at all (after time t).

($T2$) X never did A deliberately (after time t).

and are thus the two given commands *prima facie* different. But how (it might be asked) is such a difference between (1) and (2) to be reconciled with our thesis that the only proper candidates for command requirements are matters within the sphere of our control? The answer is simply this — that there are many things within our control envisaged (and forbidden) by command (1) but disregarded in (2). For example, (1), unlike (2), enjoins X not to 'allow himself to be put into a position' where he might do A *unwittingly* or *inadvertently* or *unintentionally*, etc.

5.3. Alternative Machinery: A Retrospect. In section 4 of Chapter Three we pointed out deficiencies in the 'operator analysis' of commands, e.g., of

X, do A! $\cong$ [X ! A/(*)]; say 'Smith close the door!'

as

X ! (X does A) $\cong$ X, make it true that X does A; say 'Smith, *make it true that* Smith closes the door!'

The operator analysis founders on its inability to accommodate the necessary chronological detail — e.g., it cannot handle 'X, do A whenever B happens!'. It can, however, be saved by an expedient now to be described.

56

The command $C = [X \mathbin{!} A/P]$ can be glossed as:

X, so act henceforth (after the present time t) that (at the appropriate future time) $T_t(C)$ is true!

Thus 'X, close the door!' would be construed as 'X, so act that by time $t + \Delta$ (supposing it is now time t) it will be true that X has closed the door since t-time!'. And similarly the command 'X, always speak softly to Aunty whenever you speak to her!' would be construed as 'X, so act that *by the time you die* it will be true that X has always spoken softly to Aunty whenever he spoke to her after time t (supposing it is now time t)!'.

Thus a command $C = [X \mathbin{!} A/P]$ supposed as given at time t can be presented in terms of the operator analysis as

$$X \mathbin{!} T_i^*(C)$$

where $T_t^*(C)$ *is the appropriate futuristic rephrasing of the command termination statement* $T_t(C)$.

It thus appears that the 'operator analysis' of commands can indeed be made viable, but only by introducing chronological complications whose very complexity suggests the preferability of our more direct approach.

5.4. The Role of Command Termination. The logical theory of commands whose development we shall now — after these prolonged preliminaries — shortly get under way will rest primarily on the concept of command-termination rather than on that of obedience.

The reason for this is that the notion of 'obedience' is so intricate, intentional, and conceptually untractable that it is prudent and advantageous to press the analysis as far as possible without resort to it. We want to be able to say, for example, that the command

(1) 'Smith, open box A and box B!'

obviously 'entails' in some reasonably nonproblematic sense the command

(2) 'Smith, open box A!'

Now in terms of command-termination, the relationship between (1) and (2) is easily framed: (1) cannot possibly be terminated without ensuring the termination of (2). But in terms of obedience the situation is very cumbersome. Patently Smith can *obey* command (1) without *obeying* (2), which may well not have been 'given'. What must be said is something like: 'Smith cannot obey (1) without creating a situation of such a kind that, had he been responding to command (2) in place of (1), then it would also, in that event, be proper to say that he had obeyed (2)'. It seems clear that this complex and 'iffy' sort of analysis should be avoided insofar as such avoidance is at all possible. The concept of command termination affords us a way of realizing this prospect.

For another illustration of the convenience of termination as compared with obedience consider the command: 'Somebody close the door!' This *prima facie* collective command can plausibly (and I think properly) be glossed as a distributive command[3], i.e., a

---

[3] This is typical of collective commands and is in part the reason why we do not here accord them more extensive special consideration.

cluster of commands, one addressed to each member X_1 of the group of addressees $\{X_1, X_2, \ldots, X_n\}$, each having the form

> $[X_1$! not letting it occur that no one in the group $X_1, X_2, \ldots, X_n$ closes the door/(*)]

Note that if nobody closes the door so that it remains open then every member of the group has disobeyed the initial command (i.e., has disobeyed his share of the command-cluster). And if somebody closes the door then every member of the group has 'done his bit'. The obedience-situation is rather complex, and added complexities enter in when (say) the wind blows the door shut. But the termination-situation is simple: the command being terminated or not according as the statement 'Someone (in the group $\{X_1, X_2, \ldots, X_n\}$) has closed the door' is or is not true.

5.5. Command Preclusion and Preemption. Given the concept of command termination, two useful concepts can be introduced:

(i) A fact F will be said to *preclude* the command C as of time t if the statement that F is incompatible with $T_t(C)$. Analogously a statement S may be said to *preclude* the command C as of t if S is incompatible with $T_t(C)$.

(ii) A command C_1 may be said to be *T-inconsistent* (termination inconsistent) with a command C_2 when $T_t(C_1)$ precludes command C_2 as of t, i.e., when $T_t(C_1)$ and $T_t(C_2)$ are mutually incompatible. A command may be said to *preempt* those commands that are *T*-inconsistent with itself.

59

Some examples are in order. The command 'Smith, take a walk every day!' is precluded for *d*-day by the *fact* that Smith does not take a walk on $(d + 3)$ day; and also by the *statement*: 'Smith does not take a walk on $(d + 3)$ day'. And the first-indicated command is *T*-inconsistent with the command 'Smith, never take a walk on Sundays!'

The preceding examples, in which the *T*-inconsistent commands are addressed to the same recipient, represent what might be called 'orthodox' *T*-inconsistency. Another kind of *T*-inconsistency, let us call it 'agency-exclusion', is at issue when the commands are addressed to different recipients, as for example:

Tom, eat the one and only apple in this room!

Bob, eat the one and only apple in this room!

It is an item of incidental interest that the two commands

(1) Don't ever do A!! $\cong [- \; ! \sim A/*]$

(2) Do B whenever you do A!! $\cong [- \; ! \; B/\text{you do } A]$

are *T*-consistent with one another, since the corresponding termination statements (with $X = $ you)

($T1$) X has never done A

($T2$) X has done B whenever X has done A

are not mutually inconsistent. Commands of this sort can be given with complete logical propriety, as for example, 'Do not do A, but if you should persist in

doing it despite this order of mine, then be sure to do
B!' The discrete representation for this entire command complex is:

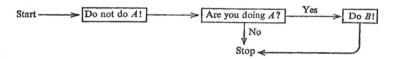

In assertoric logic, whenever p and q are inconsistent
we are entitled to infer $\sim q$ (validly) as conclusion
given p as a premiss. This has no simple analogue in
the case of commands. Thus the fact

$$F = \text{You do not do } A \text{ now}$$

precludes the command

$$C = \text{Do } A! \cong [\,-\,!\,A/(*)]$$

but we cannot infer $\sim F$ from not-C (whatever that
might be), nor conversely.

Chapter Six

COMMAND COVERAGE AND DECOMPOSITION

6.1. Orientation. The central problem for any adequate logical theory of commands is the articulation of a semantical conception of (valid) inference, on the basis of which one command can be said to be *entailed* or *implied* by (one or more) others. Before turning to this key issue, we shall first develop a conception of command coverage, which is to serve us as a conceptual model or paradigm for valid command inference. Command coverage is to serve as a means of facilitating our approach to the troublesome problem of the concept of *validity* in the 'inference' of one command from another.

6.2. Machinery. First some preliminary notions and notations. We shall use:

(i) '$\subset$' to represent the (standard) subset relation obtaining between sets, and

(ii) '$\rightarrow$' to represent (standard) logical entailment between (assertoric) propositions.

Command Coverage and Decomposition

These two notions are assumed to be familiar from other contexts and in any case present no special difficulties here. We shall furthermore use:

(iii) '$<$' to represent the relationship of *inclusion* ('being embraced in') among two actions or courses of action.

Essentially '$A_1 < A_2$' amounts to 'the doing (or carrying out) of A_2 calls for the doing (or carrying out) of A_1', or with somewhat greater precision:

(x) [(x has realized A_2) $\to$ (x has realized A_1)]

For an example of this sort of inclusion among actions let A_2 be 'removing all the books from the shelf' and A_1 be 'removing all the French books from the shelf', or let A_2 be 'seeing to it that all the doors are closed' and A_1 be 'seeing to it that the front door is closed'.

6.3. Command Coverage. Given two commands $C_1 = [X_1 \mathbin{!} A_1/P_1]$ and $C_2 = [X_2 \mathbin{!} A_2/P_2]$, we shall say that C_1 *covers* C_2 whenever the following conditions *all* obtain:

(i) $X_2 = X_1$ if the commands are addressed to individuals, or $X_2 \subset X_1$ if the commands are addressed (distributively) to groups.

(ii) $A_2 < A_1$.

(iii) $P_2 \to P_1$.

Put into words, command C_1 covers command C_2 if they differ merely in ways which satisfy the following requirements: (1) the group of addressees of C_1 includes all those of C_2; (2) C_1 calls for realizing (doing) everything which C_2 calls for realizing (doing), though possibly requiring for something additional thereto; and (3) every time at and condition under which C_2 becomes operative is also a time at and condition under which C_1 becomes operative. It is important to remark that these three conditions guarantee the transitivity of coverage.

Some illustrative instances of command coverage are as follows (the first member of each pair covering the second):

- (1a) Each of you students in this room open your books now!
- (1b) Each of you male students in this room open your books now!

- (2a) John, remove all the books from the table!
- (2b) John, remove this book [i.e., some specific one of them] from the table!

- (3a) Tom, write Jim every Wednesday in October!
- (3b) Tom, write Jim the first Wednesday in October!

- (4a) Jack, always be nice to Bob!!
- (4b) Jack, be nice to Bob when next you encounter him!

Thus far we have dealt solely with the case of one single command covering another. Coverage by several commands will obtain in the special case of a command-chain, namely a group of two (or *mutatis mutandis* more) commands either of the type,

64

Command Coverage and Decomposition

(I)   (a)   [X ! doing A/X does B][1]

      (b)   [X ! doing B/X does C]

or of type,

(II)   (a)   [X ! realizing state A/state B is realized]

      (b)   [X ! realizing state B/state C is realized]

[1] Within this pattern we also envisage such 'phased-sequence commands' as:

      [X ! doing A at $t + T/X$ does B at t]

or

      [X ! doing A at $t + T/B$ occurs at t]

By means of this machinery, we can represent a 'command program' such as 'X *do* A *every day until* B *happens and then do* C *and* D *on alternate days until* E *happens*!', represented in the 'flow-diagram':

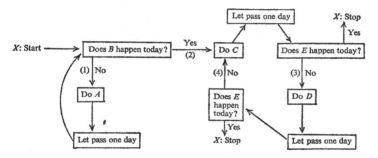

This command program can be decomposed into four commands, one corresponding to each designated point of entry into an 'instruction-execution-box':

(1)   [X ! doing A today/B has not yet happened]

(2)   [X ! doing C today/(B happens today)]

(3)   [X ! doing D today/X did C yesterday and E has not yet happened]

(4)   [X ! doing C today/X did D yesterday and E has not yet happened]

65

In these cases, we shall stipulate that the command pair (I*a*)–(I*b*) covers the command

(I*c*) [*X* ! doing *A*/*X* does *C*]

and that the pair (II*a*)–(II*b*) covers the command

(II*c*) [*X* ! realizing state *A*/state *C* is realized]

6.4. Command Coverage and Command Termination.
An important feature of command coverage must be remarked. It is clear that *in every case if the covering command(s) has (have) been terminated, it follows necessarily (by standard, assertoric logic) that the covered command has also been terminated.* This is a most significant characteristic of command coverage. To take but one illustration, the commands '*X*, do *A* whenever you do *B*!!' and '*X*, do *B* whenever you do *C*!!' lead to the termination-statements:

X has done *A* whenever *X* has done *B*

and

X has done *B* whenever *X* has done *C*

which obviously entail

X has done *A* whenever *X* has done *C*

which is the termination-statement for the command '*X*, do *A* whenever you do *C*!!'.

6.5. Contextual Coverage. It will prove important for our subsequent purposes to make one extension in the notion of command coverage to include a concept of *contextual* coverage. Given the commands $C_1 = [X_1 ! A_1/P_1]$ and $C_2 = [X_2 ! A_2/P_2]$ we shall say that C_1 *covers* C_2 *in the context of the assertoric statements*

66

$S_1, S_2, \ldots, S_n$ provided that the following conditions all obtain (where S is the conjunction $S_1 \& S_2 \& \ldots \& S_n$):

(i') Either (i) as in section 6.3 above, or we have that $X_2 \subset X_1$ given that (or: *under the condition that*) S, i.e.:

$$(x) [(S \& x \in X_2) \to x \in X_1]$$

(ii') Either (ii) as above, or we have that $(A_2 < A_1)$ given that S, i.e.:

$$(x) ([S \& (x \text{ has realized } A_1)] \to [x \text{ has realized } A_2])$$

(iii') Either (iii) as above, or we have that $P_2 \to P_1$ given that S, i.e.:

$$(S \& P_2) \to P_1$$

Thus, for example, the command

(5a) Robert, go to the largest grocer in Oxford!

covers (and is covered by) the command

(5b) Robert, go to Grimbly Hughes!

in the context of the (assertoric) statement: 'Grimbly Hughes is the largest grocer in Oxford'. For given that Grimbly Hughes = the largest grocer in Oxford, the requirement 'going to Grimbly Hughes' entails (and is indeed equivalent with) the requirement 'going to the largest grocer in Oxford'[2]. Again, in the context of the assertoric statement 'All persons in this room are male', the command

(6a) All males in this room do A!

[2] Compare the discussion of this example in *Hare* (1952), pp. 34–35.

covers the command

(6b) All persons in this room do A!

For given the assertoric statement in question we have it that the set of persons-in-this-room is included in the set of males-in-this-room. Finally, in the context of the assertoric statement 'Whenever P, then Q' the command

(7a) X, do A whenever P-and-Q!!

covers the command

(7b) X, do A whenever P!![3]

This notion of contextual coverage applies only in case of one single command covering another. (It does not extend to command chains.)

6.6. Command Decomposition. We introduce three steps by which a command may be decomposed into two others:

(1) *Addressee Decomposition*

The command $C = [Y \; ! \; A/P]$ will be said to be *addressee-decomposed* (A-*decomposed* for short) into the pair of commands $C_1 = [Y_1! \; A_1/P_1]$ and $C_2 = [Y_2 \; ! \; A_2/P_2]$ if the following three conditions are all satisfied:

(i) $Y = Y_1 \cup Y_2$

(ii) $A = A_1 = A_2$ [where $A_1 = A_2$ stands for $(A_1 < A_2) \; \& \; (A_2 < A_1)$]

---

[3] We could — but shall not — introduce a concept of 'inductive coverage' as in the move from (7a) to (7b) in the face of the assertoric statement 'Whenever P, then almost always Q'. In general, we ignore throughout the possibility of inductive kinds of inferences involving commands.

(iii) $P \leftrightarrow P_1 \leftrightarrow P_2$ [4]

(2) *Requirement Decomposition*
The command $C = [Y \; ! \; A/P]$ will be said to be *requirement-decomposed* (R-*decomposed* for short) into the pair of commands $C_1 = [Y_1 \; ! \; A_1/P_1]$ and $C_2 = [Y_2 \; ! \; A_2/P_2]$ if the following three conditions are all satisfied:

(i) $Y = Y_1 = Y_2$
(ii) $A = (A_1 \; \& \; A_2)$
(iii) $P \leftrightarrow P_1 \leftrightarrow P_2$

(3) *Precondition Decomposition*
The command $C = [Y \; ! \; A/P]$ will be said to be *precondition-decomposed* (P-*decomposed* for short) into the pair of commands $C_1 = [Y_1 \; ! \; A_1/P_1]$ and $C_2 = [Y_2 \; ! \; A_2/P_2]$ if the following three conditions are all satisfied:

(i) $Y = Y_1 = Y_2$
(ii) $A = A_1 = A_2$
(iii) $P \leftrightarrow (P_1 \vee P_2)$

The command C will be said to be *decomposed* (simpliciter) into the commands $C_1, C_2, \ldots, C_n$ if the C_i are a (complete and residueless) list of commands resulting from decomposing (in any manner) either C itself, or commands resulting from decompositions of C.

---

[4] Note that the commands 'John and Tom, move that table across the room together!' and 'John and Tom, each of you take out a pencil!' differ in that the first cannot be A-decomposed, whereas the second can.

Command Coverage and Decomposition

To put this idea into a more verbalized formulation: command C is decomposed into the pair C_1 and C_2 if it can be regarded as 'being made up of' the *conjoining* of these two commands in a 'set of orders'. Thus for example the command

$C =$ John, write to Tim and Tom every Wednesday in October! (That is: John write to Tim and to Tom today, whenever today is a Wednesday in October!)

can be R-decomposed into the pair consisting of

$C_1 =$ John, write to Tim every Wednesday in October!

together with

$C_2 =$ John, write to Tom every Wednesday in October!

The first of these two commands, i.e., C_1, can in its turn be P-decomposed into the pair consisting of:

$C_3 =$ John, write to Tim the first three Wednesdays of this October!

and

$C_4 =$ John, write to Tim the last three Wednesdays of this October!

The original command C could now be said to have been decomposed into the commands C_2, C_3, C_4 — and of course further (or other) decompositions would be possible.

It should be remarked that a command *covers* every command that figures in its decomposition. As a result, a command cannot be terminated unless all of its decomposition-commands are terminated.

Command Coverage and Decomposition

The preceding discussion of (absolute) command decomposition is readily extended to the case of contextual command decomposition in the face (context) of given assertoric statements. Thus, for example, given the assertoric statement 'Jim and Bob are the only men in the room', the command 'All men in the room, do A!' is (contextually) addressee-decomposable into the pair: 'Jim, do A!' and 'Bob, do A!'

* * *

As was remarked at the outset of this chapter, command coverage is to serve us as the guiding paradigm of valid command inference. It follows on this conception that whenever a command figures in the decomposition of a given command, it is to be regarded as entailed by (or validly inferable from) this original command.

Chapter Seven

VALIDITY AND INVALIDITY

7.1. The Problem of Validity in Command Inference.
By a 'command inference' we shall understand an argument whose conclusion is a command, and whose premisses include commands and possibly also assertoric statements. The inference will be characterized as *homogeneous* when the premisses contain only commands, and as *heterogeneous* when assertoric premisses are also present. The case of homogeneous command inference is of special interest because the command premisses correspond to the ordinary idea of a *set of instructions*, and there are of course many familiar situations in which the question of what non-explicit commands 'follow' from a set of instructions in the sense of being implicitly contained in it.

How, exactly, is one to specify the conditions and circumstances under which an 'inference' involving commands is to count as *valid?* This semantical question is surely the key problem of the logical theory of commands. Before we turn to it, a brief digression is necessary.

7.2. 'Hare's Thesis' and 'Poincaré's Principle'. Our definition of 'command inference' fails to recognize the possibility of an inference from command premisses to an assertoric conclusion. But this is a mere optical, or rather verbal, illusion. We do not gainsay the possibility of such inference, but merely withhold from it the 'command inference' label.

R. M. Hare has endorsed the rule:

No indicative conclusion can be validly drawn from a set of (indicative *cum* imperative) premisses which cannot validly be drawn from the indicatives among them alone[1].

We shall have occasion later (once a concept of 'validity' has been articulated) to reject the applicability of this general rule — let us call it 'Hare's Thesis' — to the special case we have in hand here, namely that of commands. (See section 1 of Chapter Eight.) We shall recognize as valid certain types of inference from command premisses to assertoric conclusions. Arguments of this kind have been left out of the province of 'command inference', not because we adopt Hare's Thesis that they cannot possibly be valid, but because on our view they represent a non-central side issue in the logic of commands.

In 1919 the great French mathematician and philosopher of science Henri Poincaré — arguing against the positivist project of founding morality on science — wrote:

[1] *Hare* (1952), p. 28. It should be said that Hare limits this rule to categorical imperatives, and exempts hypothetical imperatives. He writes that the 'sentence "If you want to go to the largest grocer in Oxford, go to Grimbly Hughes". . . seems to follow from, and to say no more than: "Grimbly Hughes is the largest grocer in Oxford" ' (p. 34). On this thesis compare also *Bergström* (1962*b*), especially pp. 47–48.

Il ne peut pas y avoir de morale scientifique; mais il ne peut pas y avoir non plus de science immorale. Et la raison en est simple; c'est une raison, comment dirai-je? purement grammaticale.

Si les prémisses d'un syllogisme sont toutes les deux à l'indicatif, la conclusion sera également à l'indicatif. Pour que la conclusion peût être mise à l'impératif, il faudrait que l'une des prémisses au moins fût elle-même à l'impératif. Or, les principes de la science, les postulate de la géométrie sont et ne peuvent être qu'à l'indicatif; c'est encore à ce même mode que sont les vérités expérimentales, et à la base des sciences, il n'y a, il ne peut y avoir rien autre chose. Dès lors, le dialecticien le plus subtil peut jongler avec ces principes comme il voudra, les combiner, les échafauder les uns sur les autres; tout ce qu'il en tirera sera à l'indicatif. Il n'obtiendra jamais une proposition qui dira: fais ceci, ou ne fais pas cela; c'est-à-dire une proposition qui confirme ou qui contredise la morale[2].

Poincaré here clearly articulates the rule — let it be called Poincaré's Principle — that (in R. M. Hare's formulation):

No imperative conclusion can be validly drawn from a set of (indicative *cum* imperative) premisses which does not contain at least one imperative[3].

---

[2] *Poincaré* (1913), p. 225.

[3] *Hare* (1952), p. 28. This thesis, as defended in *Dubislav* (1937), provided considerable impetus to subsequent discussions of the logic of commands.

74

This rule — essentially the converse of Hare's Thesis — will be seen later (once a concept of 'validity' is in hand) to hold good in the special case of command inferences. And this result is only to be expected, since assertoric statements fail to provide various essentials of commands (source, addressee, etc.).

7.3. 'Jørgensen's Dilemma' and 'Menger's Fable'. The problem he characterized as 'Jørgensen's Dilemma' was described by Alf Ross in the following terms:

This is the dilemma: According to the usually accepted definition of a [valid] logical inference [viz. as one whose conclusion must be true when its premisses are true], an imperative is precluded from being a constituent part of such an inference ['since an imperative, for example "close the door", can obviously be neither true nor false']. Nevertheless instances may be given of inferences the logical evidence of which seems obvious [e.g. Love your neighbor as yourself; love yourself; therefore love your neighbor] in spite of the fact that imperatives form part of them. And, further, those instances must be considered typical of the way in which reasoning actually takes place in practical life . . .[4]

In developing a theory of valid command inference we would therefore be well advised to be prepared to dispense with the straightforward considerations regarding truth and falsity that form the mainstay of the analysis in the case of assertoric inference.

Various writers, however, eager to bring the orthodox assertoric notion of validity to bear, have stood

[4] *Ross* (1939), p. 32. See also *Bergström* (1962*b*), p. 32.

ready to assign (assertoric) truth values to commands or so to construe (or reconstrue) their meaning that the assignment of truth-values to them would become natural. This course was first taken in *Menger* (1939) (where, however, a third neutral truth-value is introduced: 'doubtful', i.e., indeterminate or unknown)[5]. I myself regard the assignment of truth-values to commands (alike whether two or three possibilities are admitted) as a desperate and unpalatable expedient[6]— one which, moreover, is rendered wholly unnecessary by the prospect of importing all of the truth-considerations requisite for the logic of commands over the avenue of their associated termination-statements.

Some writers wish to articulate a semantical theory of commands on the basis of the analogy that *obedience* is to commands as *truth* is to statements. (Thus *Fischer* (1962) conceives of 'obedience values' to parallel the familiar truth values.) Its basic merits notwithstanding[7], this approach ignores aspects of the

[5] Perhaps the boldest attempt to view commands as true or false is that of *Leonard* (1959).

[6] Some of the considerations that militate against it are marshalled in *Bergström* (1962*b*), pp. 11–16 and 32–37. It was exactly the fact that commands, prayers, and questions are *not* true or false that provided the traditional line of demarcation between such non-assertoric statements on the one hand and assertoric statements on the other, ever since Aristotle (*De Interp.*, 16b33) and the Stoics (B. Mates, *Stoic Logic*, pp. 18–19).

[7] The view in question goes back at least to *Hofstadter and McKinsey* (1939). On our view its prime merit lies in giving up the vain attempt to conceive of commands as being standardly true or false, consequently according commands a genus of semantical 'values' wholly different from the standard 'truth-values' of assertoric statements.

76

concept of obedience that renders it ill-suited to serve this role. For example, a statement or proposition can clearly be true or false if no-one ever asserts it, whereas a command can manifestly not be obeyed if it is never *given*.

7.4. What Shall We Ask of 'Validity' in Command Inference? Consider the valid deductive (assertoric) inference

> All felines are mammals
> All lions are felines
> _____
> All lions are mammals

It is clear that anyone who has *overtly* asserted or accepted the premisses has thereby *implicitly* asserted or accepted the conclusion because the conclusion is tacitly or implicitly contained within the assertoric premisses. Analogously, consider the command inference

> Always say 'please' to John when you ask him for the bread!!
> Ask John for the bread now!
> _____
> Say 'please' to John now!

The inference may be characterized as 'valid' in the sense that its conclusion is tacitly or implicitly contained in its premisses so that (*inter alia*):

> (i) *Anyone* who overtly *gives* the premiss commands may legitimately claim (or be claimed) to have implicitly given the command conclusion.

(ii) *Anyone* who overtly *receives* the premiss commands may legitimately claim (or be claimed) to have implicitly received the command conclusion[8].

(iii) Any course of action on the part of their common recipient which terminates the premiss commands cannot fail to terminate the command conclusion[9].

These considerations provide at least some informal, presystematic account of the intended meaning of 'validity' in the context of command inference.

7.5. Patent Invalidity. Since we regard condition (iii) of the preceding section as a necessary condition for valid command inference we are in possession of a 'rule of rejection' for dismissing certain command inferences as invalid:

A command inference is *patently invalid* if it is possible for all of its assertoric premisses to be true and for all of its command premisses to be terminated, and yet its command conclusion to remain unterminated.

---

[8] The distinction between *actual* and *implicit* giving and *receiving* of commands circumvents the difficulties raised in *Williams* (1963) as to who is in a position to arrive at an imperative conclusion that is held to follow from imperative premisses. This entire issue of 'entitlement to infer' is masterfully dealt with in *Geach* (1963), pp. 38–40.

[9] Abstracting from the inherent complexities of the notion of 'obedience', one might give the cognate formulation that it is impossible to obey the command premisses without acting 'as if' one were obeying the command conclusion. But a long — and here unnecessary — story must be read into this 'as if'.

This rule suffices for rejecting as 'patently invalid' such an obviously invalid command inference as:

John, do A! $\cong$ [John ! $A/(*)$]
_____
John, do A and B! $\cong$ [John ! A & $B/(*)$]

7.6. Patent Validity. We now introduce the notion of *patent validity*, operative only in certain especially clear-cut cases, to provide clearer guidance in developing a more general theory of valid command inference. In doing this, we shall place essential reliance upon the concepts of command *coverage* and *decomposition* explained in Chapter Five above.

A command inference is *patently valid* if it accords with the following criterion:

The inference whose conclusion is the command C and whose premisses include the commands C_1, C_2, ..., C_n is *patently valid* if the command C can be decomposed into the set of commands $C_1^{\#}$, $C_2^{\#}$, ..., $C_m^{\#}$ in such a way that each $C_i^{\#}$ is covered by some of the C_j.

Given this concept, the following is an example of a patently valid command inference:

C_1 = John, do A and B (always)!! $\cong$
[John ! A & $B/*$]

C_2 = John, do both C and D whenever P!! $\cong$
[John ! C & D/P]
_____
C_3 = John, do both A and C whenever P!! $\cong$
[John ! A & C/P]

The validity of this inference can be exhibited as follows: The conclusion C_3 can be decomposed into the pair:

$$C_4 = [\text{John } ! \ A/P]$$
$$C_5 = [\text{John } ! \ C/P]$$

But C_4 is covered by premiss C_1, and C_5 is covered by premiss C_2.

The foregoing concept of valid command inference is readily extended to include nonhomogeneous command inferences where assertoric premisses play an essential role. Here we introduce the following criterion for contextual validity:

> The inference whose conclusion is the command C and whose premisses include the commands $C_1, C_2, \ldots, C_n$ is *valid in the context of* (or read: *contextually valid given*) the assertoric premisses $S_1, S_2, \ldots, S_m$ if the command conclusion C can be decomposed — either absolutely or in the context of $S_1, S_2, \ldots, S_m$ — into the set of commands $C_1^{\#}, C_2^{\#}, \ldots, C_k^{\#}$ in such a way that each $C_i^{\#}$ can be covered by some of the C_j either by simple coverage or by contextual coverage given the assertoric statements $S_1, S_2, \ldots, S_m$.

In contextual validity, unlike patent validity, assertoric premisses can play a vital role.

Some examples of command inferences satisfying our criterion of contextual validity are:

(I) 'X, do A when next P!'

$$\cong [X \ ! \ A/(P)]$$

P-next-now $\quad = P$-next-now

'X, do A now!' $\quad \cong [X \ ! \ A/(*)]$

(II) 'X, do A whenever P!!'

$$\cong [X \, ! \, A/P]$$

$$\frac{P\text{-now}}{\text{'}X, \text{do } A \text{ now!'}} \quad \frac{= P\text{-now}}{\cong [X \, ! \, A/(*)]}$$

(III) 'X, do A whenever P & Q!!'

$$\cong [X \, ! \, A/P \, \& \, Q]$$

$$\frac{Q\text{-always}}{\text{'}X, \text{do } A \text{ whenever } P\text{!!'}} \quad \frac{= Q\text{-always}}{\cong [X \, ! \, A/P]}$$

Particular interest attaches to the paradigm

(IV) 'X, do A whenever P!!'

$$\cong [X \, ! \, A/P]$$

$$\frac{\text{Whenever } Q, \text{ then } P}{\text{'}X, \text{do } A \text{ whenever } Q\text{!'}} \quad \frac{= \text{Whenever } Q, \text{ then } P}{\cong [X \, ! \, A/Q]}$$

It is to be remarked that no command inference that is contextually valid in the sense just given can be patently invalid in the sense specified at the outset of this section.

* * *

In the case of purely assertoric inference the notion of a 'contextually valid entailment' is a useless complication. For the question of the contextual validity of the inference

Premiss 1	Contextual Assertion 1
. . .	. . .
Premiss n	Contextual Assertion m

Conclusion

81

is nothing different from that of the standard validity of the inference

> Premiss 1
>
> . . .
>
> Premiss n
>
> Contextual Assertion 1
>
> . . .
>
> Contextual Assertion m
> _____
> Conclusion

The rewritten inference becomes a homogeneously orthodox assertoric inference. In the case of a command inference, however, the question of contextual validity in the presence of auxiliary assertoric premisses raises characteristic difficulties of its own and has therefore to be treated as a separate issue.

7.7. Validity in Homogeneous Command Inference. We must now take up the problem of the validity of command inferences in a more general way. We begin by confining our attention to the homogeneous case, in which only commands (and no assertoric statements) are present among the premisses. Several preliminary ideas must first be introduced.

A *scenario* for a command is a combination of (i) a complete *possible* biography of its recipient (subsequent to the hypothetical 'time-of-giving' of the command) with respect to those items of behaviour and of occurrence that are at issue in the command, together with (ii) a complete *possible* history of the subsequent course of relevant (extra-biographical) events. Thus a scenario for the command 'John, always carry an umbrella on rainy days!!' is a characterization for all days (of John's subsequent life) indicating for each day whether or not it rained and whether or not John carried an umbrella. In general — again resuming our discrete-time model — a scenario for the command $[X! \ A/P]$ would be given as a tabulation of the following kind:

time	t_0	$t_0 + u$
state-of-affairs	P obtains	P does not obtain
action/realization	X does (realizes) A	X does not do (realize) A

$t_0 + 2u$	$t_0 + 3u$	
P obtains	P obtains	
X does do (realize) A	X does not do (realize) A	

A scenario will be said to *bypass* a command if, when it is assumed that it represents the actual course of events, the precondition under which the command becomes operative simply *does not arise*. A scenario will be said to *satisfy* a command if, when it is assumed that it represents the actual course of events, the command is not only not bypassed, but it would moreover be correct to say that the recipient has *terminated* the command. Thus, in the preceding example, the indicated scenario does *not* satisfy the command $[X! \ A/P]$ because it indicates that at time $t_0 + 3u$, P did obtain but X did not do (realize) A, so that the termination statement 'X did (realized) A whenever P'

would be incorrect (false). A scenario will be said to *violate* a command which it not only does not bypass, but whose *nontermination* is assured by it.

The set of commands $C_1, C_2, \ldots, C_n$ will be said to *entail* (validly) the command conclusion C if

   (i) No scenario that satisfies all the premisses can possibly violate the conclusion (although it may bypass it), and

  (ii) When there are scenarios that satisfy all the premisses, then some of them do not bypass the conclusion.

Putting the matter more informally (and somewhat more inexactly) we may say that a command conclusion is validly inferred from a certain group of command premisses if every possible world in which all the premisses are terminated will also have to be such that the conclusion is terminated.

Thus, for example, the command 'Tom, write Jim every Wednesday in October!' entails the command 'Tom, write Jim the first Wednesday in October!'

7.8. Examples of Valid and Invalid Homogeneous Command Inferences. The following homogeneous command inferences are all valid entailments:

$$[-\ !\ A/P]$$
$$[-\ !\ B/P]$$
$$\overline{[-\ !\ A\ \&\ B/P]}^{10}$$

---

[10] Certain A's and B's seemingly cannot be conjoined indifferently. For example: 'If he comes, bid him welcome!' and 'If he comes, go to the door to let him in!' The moves called for here are familiar from assertoric logic.

$$[- \; ! \; A/R]$$
$$[- \; ! \; A/S]$$
$$\overline{[- \; ! \; A/R \text{ v } S]}$$

$$[- \; ! \; A/P]$$
$$[- \; ! \; B/P \; \& \; Q]$$
$$\overline{[- \; ! \; A \; \& \; B/P \; \& \; Q]}$$

$[- \; !$ doing $A/$you (i.e., the addressee) do $B]$
$[- \; !$ doing $B/$you do $C]$
$\overline{[- \; !$ doing $A/$you do $C]}$

$$[- \; ! \; A/(\text{you do } B)]$$
$$[- \; ! \; B/(*)]$$
$$\overline{[- \; ! \; A/(*)]}^{11}$$

$[- \; !$ realizing state $A/$state B is realized]
$[- \; !$ realizing state $B/$state C is realized]
$\overline{[- \; !$ realizing state $A/$state C is realized]}$

Some examples of invalid command inferences are:

$$[- \; ! \; A/R]$$
$$[- \; ! \; B/Q]$$
$$\overline{[- \; ! \; A \; \& \; B/R]}$$

$$[- \; ! \; A/R]$$
$$[- \; ! \; B/S]$$
$$\overline{[- \; ! \; A \; \& \; B/R \text{ v } S]}$$

An interesting case of invalidity is that of the immediate inference

---

[11] The validity of this inference, i.e., 'If (i.e., when next) you do B, do A; do B now; do A now!', is denied in *Castaneda* (1958), but on grounds whose insufficiency is rightly noted in Bennett's review.

$$\frac{C_1 = X, \text{ never do } A!! \cong [X \mathbin{!} \sim A/\text{*}]}{C_2 = X, \text{ do } B \text{ whenever you do } A!!}$$
$$\cong [X \mathbin{!} B/X \text{ does } A]$$

On the proposed conception of 'validity' this inference is invalid, because *every* scenario that satisfies C_1 will have to bypass (rather than satisfy) C_2. (Note, however, that this inference would be valid if clause (ii) were dropped from our definition of 'validity'.) A similar analysis holds for the command inference

$$\frac{\text{Do } A \text{ (now)}! \cong [- \mathbin{!} \text{doing } A/(\text{*})]}{\text{If you do not (now) do } A, \text{ do } B!}$$
$$\cong [- \mathbin{!} \text{doing } B/(\text{you do not now do } A)]$$

It may be remarked that this (invalid) inference is the command counterpart of the 'paradox' of implication

$$\frac{p}{\text{If not-}p, \text{ then } q}$$

A particularly common pattern of valid command inference arises when A, B, and C are such that the following command inference is valid:

$$\frac{[- \mathbin{!} A \mathbin{\&} B/(\text{*})]}{[- \mathbin{!} C/(\text{*})]}$$

For in this case the general validity of

$$\frac{[- \mathbin{!} A/\text{*}]}{[- \mathbin{!} B/(\text{*})]}$$
$$\overline{[- \mathbin{!} A \mathbin{\&} B/(\text{*})]}$$

underwrites the validity of

$$\frac{[- \mathbin{!} A/\text{*}]}{[- \mathbin{!} B/(\text{*})]}$$
$$\overline{[- \mathbin{!} C/(\text{*})]}$$

Two examples of valid command inferences of this type are:

> Make an abstract of every book you read!! ≅ [— !
> abstracting every book you read/*]
> Read every book on the shelf! ≅ [— ! reading every
> book on the shelf/(*)]
> ___
> Make an abstract of every book on the shelf!
> ≅ [— ! abstracting every book on the shelf/(*)]

> *X*, always say 'please' to anyone when asking him
> for anything!! ≅ [*X*! saying 'please' to everyone
> you ask for anything/*]
> *X*, ask John for the bread! ≅ [*X*! asking John for
> the bread/(*)]
> ___
> *X*, say 'please' to John! ≅ [*X*! saying 'please' to
> John/(*)]

Both of these arguments fall into the generic pattern described above.

The 'standard' case of command inference, and certainly the one we usually have in mind when thinking of a *set of instructions*, is clearly that in which all the commands at issue are addressed to a single common addressee. However, we have not built this into our 'logic', and in fact we must be prepared (by our specified criterion of validity) to recognize as valid such 'mixed-addressee' command inferences as:

> Tom, be pleasant to everyone who speaks to you!!
> John, speak to Tom!
> ___
> Tom, be pleasant to John!

This case is, however, a non-standard one, for in the validity-analysis of such commands we must of course have resort to multi-person scenarios.

7.9. Observations on the Preceding Concept of Validity.
We have articulated the concept of *command inference* in such a way as to call for an explicit admission that the notion of 'validity'— and indeed of 'inference' itself — have undergone a meaning shift in the move from assertoric logic. Anyone minded to object to this must bear in mind the fact that these concepts also undergo a meaning-shift (albeit a less drastic one) in the move from one branch of assertoric logic to another — e.g., from propositional logic to quantificational logic. This point is readily seen by comparing and contrasting the valid inferences

$$\frac{p \ \& \ q}{p} \qquad\qquad \frac{(x) \ Fx}{Fa}$$

drawn from propositional and quantificational logic, respectively.

In any case, we do not want to gloss over the fact that the move from assertoric to command logic does require a genuine 'redeployment of terms' of somewhat the same kind as is the case with 'addition' and 'division' in the move from integers to rational numbers, and again from the rationals to the reals.

Our characterization of the 'validity' of homogeneous command inferences is in any case simply transformed from the usual semantical characterization of validity in quantificational logic, to wit: *A quantificational inference is valid if there is no possible world in which the premisses are all true and the conclusion fails to be true.* We have adapted this characterization with but one change:

A command inference is valid if there is no possible world in which the premisses are all satisfied and the conclusion fails to be satisfied.

The sole change here is the substitution of 'satisfied' for 'true'[12] (the notion of 'possible world' remains specifically the same), surely neither a greatly surprising nor an unduly drastic change in the wake of a shift from the logic of assertion to that of commands.

Finally, it should be noted that — termination statements being assertoric in character — our characterization of validity for homogeneous command inferences carries the entire issue back into purely assertoric logic[13].

7.10. Variant Conceptions of Validity. It is useful and illuminating to re-examine the proposed definition of *validity* in command inference in the light of related alternatives[14]. Consider the following family of definitions:

The inference of the command-conclusion C from the command premisses $C_1, C_2, \ldots, C_n$ is valid if it is the case for every possible scenario that:

When all the premisses are:	the conclusion must be:
(A) satisfied	satisfied

[12] This is strictly speaking not quite accurate because we have adapted the characterization from the two-valued true/false situation to one that is three-valued satisfied/bypassed/violated. The formula should end with the words: *satisfied or bypassed.*

[13] The general line of approach taken here in defining validity in command inference in terms not of the 'truth' or 'falsity' of commands, but of the interrelationships of certain assertoric counterparts of commands, goes back at least to *Jørgensen* (1937–38). See (unsympathetic) summary given in *Ross* (1941).

[14] This section owes an especially heavy debt to my colleague, Professor Nuel D. Belnap, Jr.

(B) satisfied   non-violated

(C) non-violated   non-violated

(E) (Conjunction of (A) and (C), i.e., both must be the case)

(F) (Disjunction of (A) and (C), i.e., one must be the case)

These characterizations of validity are related as follows:

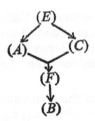

where the arrow is such that '$(U) \to (V)$' means 'An inference valid according to (U) is necessarily valid according to (V)'.

Now it must be noted that, in view of our adoption of command coverage as a paradigm of validity in command inference, we are committed to the validity of the inference

$$\frac{[X \mathbin{!} A/P] \cong X, \text{do } A \text{ whenever } P!!}{[X \mathbin{!} A/P \mathbin{\&} Q] \cong X, \text{do } A \text{ whenever } P \text{ and } Q!!}$$

But here it can certainly occur that for some scenarios the command premiss is satisfied and the conclusion not be satisfied (by being bypassed). This rules out

90

our adoption of definition (A) — and *à fortiori* (E) — as placing too strong restrictions upon validity.

On the other hand, we wish to reject as invalid the surely objectionable inference-pattern

$$\frac{[X \mathbin{!} A/P]}{[X \mathbin{!} B/P \text{ and } X \text{ does not do } A]}$$

But this inference will be valid according to definition (C) — and *à fortiori* (F) and (B) — since wherever the premiss is either satisfied or bypassed the conclusion is automatically bypassed.

Seemingly we have reached a dead end, having found definitions (A)–(F) all unacceptable. However, the situation is not so grave as it seems because of the extreme peculiarity of the last-considered inference in that the premisses and the conclusion are not possibly jointly satisfiable. Hence we would be free to adopt definition (C) — and *à fortiori* (F) and (B) — if we added the qualifying clause

with the proviso that when the premisses are jointly satisfiable at all, then the inference be deemed invalid if they are not *jointly satisfiable with the conclusion*.

We thus have three alternatives open to us, namely (C'), (F'), and (B') the qualified counterparts to (C), (F), and (B), respectively. They are related as follows:

$$(C') \rightarrow (F') \rightarrow (B')$$

with the arrow to be understood in line with the preceding explanation. We have adopted (B') because it provides (in view of these interrelationships) the least restrictive of these conceptions of validity, and affords the largest scope for valid command inference.

Chapter Eight

VALIDITY IN MIXED CASES

8.1. Inference from Command Premisses to an Assertoric Conclusion: Presupposition Inferences. We have defined a *command inference* in such a way that its conclusion must be a command. But it will not do to overlook completely the case of inferences that derive an *assertoric* conclusion from premisses among which commands figure in an essential way.

It would seem plausible to maintain, for example, that an immediate inference from a command premiss to a conclusion that represents a *presupposition* of this command should be regarded as valid. Instances of this are

John, drive your car home!
_____
John owns a car.

John, go to the grocery on the corner!
_____
There is a grocery on the corner.

Such commands of the type, 'John, stop beating your wife!' can be analyzed as a *meshed composite of an assertion and a command*, as follows:

John, you own a car: drive it home!
John, there is a grocery on the corner: go there!

John, you have a wife and have been beating her:
stop beating her!

And obviously, the assertoric component of such a
'meshed composite' can be viewed as extractable by an
'inference'[1]. This, of course, also opens up the possibility of mediate inference by combining the assertoric
components of several commands, e.g., of inferring
from the two previously indicated commands the
conclusion 'John is a married car-owner' (i.e., John is
married *and* John owns a car).

* * *

In *von Wright* (1963) the logic of commands is
approached from the angle of 'change-logic' based on
expressions of the form

$$p \, T \, q$$

which are to be understood as '(the state of affairs
characterized by the proposition) p changes to (the
state of affairs characterized by the proposition) q'[2].
To this basic idea von Wright adds (in different
notation) two command operators, C^+ and C^-, such
that

$$C^+ (p \, T \, q)$$
$$C^- (p \, T \, q)$$

are to be construed (respectively) as

It is commanded to change p to q!
It is commanded not to change p to q!

---

[1] It will be recalled, however, that we adopt the convention that
when its assertoric constituent is false, the composite is — not
false, but — inappropriate or meaningless.

[2] We use 'change' here in an artificial, technical sense; indeed q
may be the same as p so that no actual change is involved at
all. 'p *changes to* q' should be glossed as 'p is *succeeded* by q'.

However, the locution 'You are commanded to change *p* to *q*!' can be construed in two very different alternative ways, depending upon the chronology of the situation, viz.:

(1) p *is now the case*, change it to *q*!

(2) *Whenever* p *is the case*, change it to *q*!

With alternative (1) we are confronted by a meshed composite of exactly the type now under consideration, combining (a) the statement that *p* is now the case, with (b) the command to realize *q*. With alternative case (2), on the other hand, we have a standard conditional command of the type: [− ! realizing *q*/*p* is the case]. Von Wright's discussion leaves it unclear (so far as I can see) which of these two alternative constructions is adopted by him: sometimes his illustrations and explanations point one way, sometimes the other.

* * *

This 'meshed composite' conception of presuppositional commands can be used to exhibit the plausibility of the inference

$$\frac{X, \text{do } A \text{ when } P!! \cong [X \text{ ! } A/P]}{X \text{ can do } A \text{ when } P}$$

For the premiss command '*X*, do *A* when *P*!!' can plausibly be analyzed the meshed composite

$$X, \text{you can do } A \text{ when } P: \text{do it}!!$$

whose assertoric component yields the conclusion of the inference under consideration. Note that when the officer orders a soldier

94

Swim across the river! $\cong$ You can swim across the river: do it!

then the soldier's failure to do what is asked if he cannot swim is not — on our view — an instance of disobedience precisely because he has good grounds for claiming the inappropriateness of the command[3].

It is worth remarking that the assertoric components of two commands can be inconsistent with one another, for example:

Get married! $\cong$ you do not now have a wife: get one!

Be kind to your present wife! $\cong$ You have a wife at present: be kind to her!

Such commands are incompatible in a strong and characteristic way, and cannot be conjoined without absurdity.

One could introduce special machinery to render explicit that the command C has associated with it by way of presuppositions all consequences of the assertoric statement S_c[4]. And one can then base various derivative notions upon this idea. For example, we could introduce the definition:

Commands C_1 and C_2 are *P-inconsistent* (presupposition inconsistent) when the statements S_{c1} and S_{c2} are (assertorically) inconsistent.

(An illustration of this particular idea was already given in the last paragraph.) But we shall not pursue the prospect of such elaborations any further here.

[3] Compare *von Wright* (1963), pp. 114–115.
[4] When S_c is false we shall class the command as *absurd* (or *improper* or *incongruous*) rather than as *false*.

8.2. Inference from Command Premisses to an Assertoric Conclusion: Antilogistic Inferences. Interesting examples of a different type are:

> Always tell the truth!!
> Tell Tom that John said he would come!
> ――――――――――――――――――――――
> John said he would come

> Never do anything illegal!!
> Do A!
> ――――――――――――
> Doing A is legal

> Do A whenever and only when p is the case!!
> Do A now!
> ――――――――――――――――――――――――
> p is the case now

> Do A when and only when p is the case!!
> Do not do A now!
> ――――――――――――――――――――――――
> p is not the case now

> Talk to Miss X but to no one else!
> Talk to Robert's sister!
> ――――――――――――――――――――――
> Miss X is (the same person as) Robert's sister

The *nervus probandi* of arguments of this sort[5] seems to be that they can be validated by means of an antilogistic argument of the standard command inference type. Thus the second argument in the preceding list leads to

> Never do anything illegal!!
> Doing A is illegal
> ――――――――――――――
> Do not do A!

[5] My attention was directed to the important role of arguments of this sort — albeit not these specific examples — by Mr André Gombay.

where the (valid) command conclusion outrightly countermands the second premiss of the original argument.

Presupposition-inferences of the type considered in the preceding section must be exempted from the province of antilogistic reasoning (exactly as is the case with purely assertoric presupposition-inferences).

Recognizing as valid the inference

> John, drive your car home!
> ――――――――――――――
> John owns a car

we do not wish to permit the move to

> John does not own a car
> ――――――――――――――――
> John, do not drive your car home!

Given 'John does not have a car' the most that can legitimately be inferred is the *impropriety* of giving the initial command ('John, drive your car home!') — i.e., the need for *withdrawing* or *voiding* it—and not its *countermand*. However, these considerations lead into the topic of command negation which shall be deferred to section 2 of Chapter Nine.

A rather interesting example is afforded by the inference

(1) If you do A, do B!
(2) You cannot do B
――――――――――――
(3) Do not do A!

The validity of this inference may be exhibited as follows. We first consider the (patently valid) argument whose premisses are (1) above and the countermand of the conclusion (3):

97

 (1) If you do *A*, do *B*!

(−3) Do *A*!

 (4) Do *B*!

But (4) entails 'You can do *B*' by way of a presupposition-entailment (as above). Hence the premisses (1) and (−3) lead us, *via* conclusion (4), to (−2), whence the original argument can be validated by antilogism. This antilogistic strategy gives us a way of introducing into command inference not only straightforward assertoric statements, but modalized ones as well. But we shall not follow up this lead any further here.

Another interesting example is that of the inference:

Never lie to your parents!! ≅ [−! not telling a lie to your parents/*]

Tell your parents that *p*! ≅ [− ! telling your parents that *p*/(*)]

p is true   ≅   *p*

This inference may be validated by the following line of reasoning:

By considerations of contextual command coverage, the following inference is seen to be valid:

[−. ! not telling a lie to your parents/*]

Telling your parents now that *p* would be lying to them

[− ! not telling your parents now that *p*/*]

The conclusion can be reformulated as

[− ! not telling your parents that *p*/(*)]

Given the reformulated conclusion, the inference validates, by antilogism, the argument:

[— ! not telling a lie to your parents/*]
[— ! telling your parents that p/(*)]
___

Telling your parents now that p would not be lying
to them

By assertoric logic, the conclusion 'p is true' can be
inferred from the conclusion of the preceding argument, and the original inference is thus validated.

**8.3. Problem Cases in Heterogeneous Command
Inference.** In our preceding discussion of contextual
command coverage — viz., coverage in a suitable
context of assertoric statements — we have already
endorsed certain classes of heterogeneous (nonhomogeneous) command inferences as valid. But we
have (deliberately) given no general characterization
of validity for this case. The following condition,
however, will be put forward as necessary (albeit not
also sufficient):

A command inference that infers a command
conclusion from premisses containing a mixture of
commands and assertoric statements can be valid
only if the command conclusion must be terminated
whenever (i.e., in any possible world in which) all
the command premisses are terminated and all of
the assertoric premisses are true.

The insufficiency of this condition is shown by such
examples as

John, do A whenever you do B!!
John does in fact do C whenever B
___

John, do A and C whenever B!!

The question of what must be added to render sufficient the given necessary condition for valid command inference in the heterogeneous case is left as an open problem. We do not here put forward any *general* theory of validity for heterogeneous command inference.

One paradigm of heterogeneous command inference is of special interest, namely

Do *A*!

Doing *A* entails doing *B*
_____

Do *B*!

In standard cases this is validated in terms of command coverage (i.e., whenever $B < A$). But this fails to be the case whenever 'doing *B*' is not a genuine action — i.e., one over whose doing we can exercise deliberate control[6]. Thus the following inferences are definitely not validated by coverage considerations:

Recite *Gunga Din*!

Reciting *Gunga Din* entails being able to remember *Gunga Din*
_____

Be able to remember *Gunga Din*!

[6] This situation is analogous to what is known as the 'Good Samaritan Paradox' of deontic logic, i.e., the failure of the paradigm

It is right to bring about (the state of affairs) *A*

Realization of *A* entails realization of *B*
_____

It is right to bring about *B*

to be generally valid in the face of such counter-examples as:

It is right to bring about the existence of help to an assault victim

The existence of help to an assault victim entails the existence of an assault
_____

It is right to bring about the existence of an assault

Come to see me tomorrow!

Coming to see me tomorrow entails not being crushed by a falling meteorite in the interim

Do not get crushed by a falling meteorite before tomorrow!

8.4. A Rival Conception of Validity. The only fundamentally different promising alternative strategy of approach to the conception of validity in command inference seems to me to be that proposed by Lars Bergström[7] on the basis of a very conscientious survey of other ideas in the field. It is of special interest because of its facile general accommodation of 'mixed', nonhomogeneous inferences. Adhering to the propositional-operator approach to commands, Bergström first introduces the concept of a !-system, as follows:

A !-system *S* is a class of sentences (or judgments or propositions) satisfying the following eight conditions (read '... iff—' as '... if and only if—' and '... then—' as 'if ... then—'):

(i) $p \in S$ iff $\sim p \notin S$

(ii) $!\,p \in S$ then $!\sim p \notin S$

(iii) $(p \vee q) \in S$ iff $(p \in S$ or $q \in S)$

(iv) $(p \,\&\, q) \in S$ iff $(p \in S$ and $q \in S)$

(v) $(p \supset q) \in S$ iff $(p \notin S$ or $q \in S)$

(vi) $(p \cong q) \in S$ iff $[(p \in S$ and $q \in S)$ or $(p \notin S$ and $q \notin S)]$

(vii) $(x)\ Fx \in S$ iff For all individual constants $a, fa \in S$

---

[7] See *Bergström* (1962*b*).

(viii) $(\exists x)\, Fx \in S$ iff   For some individual constant a, $Fa \in S$.

On the basis of this conception of a !-system, Bergström proceeds to define validity for inferences involving commands as follows:

> The inference from the premisses $p, q, \ldots, r$ to the conclusion s is *valid* if and only if s must needs be a member of any and every !-system of which $p, q, \ldots, r$ are members.

This attempt to extend one of the usual conceptions of validity so as to embrace command inferences suffers from the following shortcomings:

(1) It is subject to the (already-mentioned) limitations inherent generally in the propositional operator approach.

(2) It provides insufficient guidance to the interpretation of the !-operator: the semantics of ! is left too indeterminate. Indeed this situation is so grave that there is nothing in the definitions of a !-system and of validity to preclude interpreting ! simply as negation $(\sim)$ or as truth or as falsity or as necessity or as impossibility.

(3) Conditions (i) and (ii) conjointly yield

$$! \sim p \in S \text{ then } \sim !\, p \in S$$

We are, however, not provided with enough information as to the construction of the type of expression in which negation-sign precedes a command operator. And the situation is especially puzzlesome with such commands as '$! \sim ! p$' and '$\sim !! p$'. (The negation of commands is a very complex matter, as will be seen below. *Not ordering* Y *to do* A is obviously different from *ordering* Y *not to do* A.)

(4) The proposed definition fails (so far as I can see) to validate such an inference as

$$\frac{\text{If } p \text{ then (necessarily) } q}{! q}$$

This sort of inference is not forthcoming on Bergström's approach even under special assumptions (apart from the implausible thesis that in general $! p$ is equivalent with p).

Chapter Nine

LOGICAL RELATIONS AMONG COMMANDS

9.1. Introduction. We turn now to a consideration of the logical characteristics of certain special kinds of complex commands: the command analogues to propositions compounded by means of such propositional connectives as negation, conjunction, and disjunction. In this way we shall be able to apply (rather than to extend) the conception of validity in command inference developed in the preceding chapters.

9.2. Negation and Countermand. With commands there is not — as there is with assertoric propositions — a simple and straightforward notion of negation (contradictory-formation). Several quite distinct modes of 'negation' must be considered.

In what is perhaps the most natural sense of the term, the 'negation' of a command is not a command at all. Thus

(1) Robert, go away!

would seemingly have the natural 'negation'

(2) Robert, you need not go away!

Here the 'negation' of a command is not a command at all, but an *authorization*, i.e., the giving of permission to do or not to do something. The command says that such-and-such *must* be done, its 'negation' says that this thing *need not* be done.

Thus one kind of command 'negation' revolves about what we shall call an *authorization*, a 'licence-extension' that sets the recipient at liberty to do something. We could introduce $(X : A/P)$ to be read as 'X, you are to be free to (or: *at liberty to*) realize A whenever P'. (This is not to say that 'you *are* permitted to' but rather 'you *have my* (i.e., the source's) permission to'.) Here $(X: \sim A/P)$ and $[X \ ! \ A/P]$ may be taken as a mode of contradictories to one another[1]. Note that while $[X \ ! \ A/P] \cong$ 'X, you *must* do A when P!' has *necessity* as a modal analogue, $(X: A/P) \cong$ 'X, you may do A when P!' has *possibility* as a modal analogue. Thus $(X: A/P)$ and $(X: \sim A/P)$ are in no way incompatible, exactly as with 'S is possible' and '$\sim S$ is possible'.

Given a command $C = [X \ ! \ A/P]$, we shall speak of

    (i) its *strong countermand* C^*, defined as
           $C^* = Df \quad [X \ ! \sim A/P],$

    (ii) its *weak countermand* C', defined as
           $C' = Df \quad [X \ ! \sim A/\{P\}].$

Thus the strong countermand of 'Tom, speak loudly to Aunty whenever you speak with her!!' is 'Tom, never speak loudly to Aunty when you speak with her!!' and its weak countermand is 'Tom, do not speak

---

[1] On the mutual contradictoriness of commands and permission statements see *von Wright* (1963), *passim*.

loudly to Aunty at some time that you speak with her!'
Any command will be T-inconsistent both with its
weak and its strong countermand[2].

It is clear that in the case of a when-next command
$C = [X ! A/(P)]$ the strong and weak countermands
will coincide, so that $C^* = C' \cong [X ! \sim A/(P)]$,
with the result that we can here speak simply of a
countermand simpliciter. *A fortiori* thus will be the
case with a peremptory command having the empty
condition (*). Example: 'John close the door!'—
'John don't close the door!'

The countermand of a command does not go to the
other extreme: the countermand of 'Close your eyes
tight!' is not 'Open your eyes wide!' but merely 'Do
not close your eyes tight!'.

* * *

Consider the two trios:

(1a)   Whenever you do A, do B!!

(2a)   Do not do B now!

(3a)   You do (in fact) do A now.

(1b)   Whenever you do A, do B!!

(2b)   Do A now!

(3b)   You do not (in fact) do B now.

In each case an inconsistency is involved which can
be brought out by antilogisms. In the first trio, (1a)

[2] On the other hand, even commands with one and the same
command requirement may be T-inconsistent. For example:
'Adam, eat (all of) the one and only apple on the tree!' and
'Eve, eat (all of) the one and only apple on the tree!'.

and (2a) validly entail the command conclusion 'Do not do A now!' which is precluded by the fact of (3a). Again (1a) entails — in the context of the fact (3a) — the command 'Do B now!' which countermands (2a). Also in the context of (3a) the commands (1a) and (2a) are T-inconsistent. (The situation is exactly analogous in the case of the second example.) In such instances, a countermand serves as a sort of 'negation' in antilogistic reasoning, as we saw in section 8.2.

Consider the pair of commands:

(1) If (i.e., whenever) you do A, then do B!! $\cong$ [— ! doing B/you do A]

(2) If (i.e., whenever) you do A, then do not do B!! $\cong$ [— ! not doing B/you do A]

These commands (taken conjointly as premises) are perfectly consistent, and validly yield the conclusion

(3) Do not (i.e., ever) do A!! $\cong$ [— ! not doing A/*].

This is readily shown by antilogism, adding to (1) and (2) the weak countermand of (3), viz.

(—3) Do A sometime! $\cong$ [— ! doing A/{*}]

which leads to the inconsistency: [— ! doing B and not doing B/{*}]. On the other hand (and the contrast is an interesting one), the commands

(4) If A happens[3], do B!! $\cong$ [— ! doing B/A happens]

(5) If A happens, do not do B!! $\cong$ [— ! not doing B/A happens]

are inconsistent (T-inconsistent) under the supposition that A ever happens.

---

[3] We suppose that the happening of A is something that lies outside human control.

An interesting case is afforded by the following set of instructions:

(1) Never go to Post 1 without first going to Post 2!!

(2) Only go to Post 3 after first going to Post 1!!

(3) Always go to Post 3 before you go to Post 2!!

(4) Go to Post 3!

It is readily seen that — supposing that the transit time from one post to another can never be less than some definite interval Δ^4— this set of instructions is inconsistent, since commands (1)–(3) have the consequence 'Never go to Post 3 without first going to Post 3!!' (So that we are, in effect, caught in an infinite regress by these three commands.) Thus (1)–(3) yield (by antilogism) the command 'Never go to Post 3!!'— and, by symmetry, similar prohibitions regarding Posts 1 and 2. Command (4) is inconsistent with this result.

*   *   *

Several important logical principles follow from the given definitions of countermanding. For one thing, it is clear that the inferences

---

[4] This assumption is crucial because otherwise (most strikingly if all three posts are *identical*) the infinite regress inherent (as we shall see) in commands (1)–(3) is not vicious. Consider an (infinite) set of instructions of Zenonian type: 'Never move to Point 1 without first moving to Point $\frac{1}{2}$!!', 'Never move to Point $\frac{1}{2}$ without first moving to Point $\frac{1}{4}$!!', etc. We assume these to be based on a layout of the following sort:

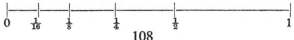

$$\frac{C^{**}}{C} \quad \text{and} \quad \frac{C}{C^{**}}$$

are valid since doing (realizing) $\sim \sim A$ amounts to doing (realizing) A (i.e., we have both $A < \sim \sim A$ and $\sim \sim A < A$).

Further, if the commands $C_1 = [X \,!\, A/P]$ and $C_2 = [X \,!\, B/P]$ are such that the inference

$$\frac{C_1}{C_2}$$

is valid, then the corresponding contrapositive inferences

$$\frac{C_2^*}{C_1^*} \quad \text{and} \quad \frac{C_2'}{C_1'}$$

must also be valid. This is so because the initial inference can be valid only when $B < A$, and when this is so, then we must have $\sim A < \sim B$.

* * *

In contraposing the command $[X \,!\, \text{do } A/\text{you do } B]$ it is also necessary to give heed to the temporal relations involved. It seems odd to move from

X, whenever (i.e., any day on which) you do A, do B the next day!!

to

X, whenever you do not do B the next day, do not do A!!

This oddity, we must insist, is more apparent and stylistic than genuine and substantive. The consequence is odd not because it is invalid, but only because this second command is formulated in what is, from the standpoint of ordinary usage, very much a 'cart before the horse' way. The inference at issue is, on our view, every bit as valid as that from

> *X*, whenever you don't pay the entrance fee first, don't go in to the exhibit!!

to

> *X*, whenever you go in to the exhibit, pay the entrance fee first!!

* * *

It should be noted that inference by *contraposition* is subject to an important restriction that has already been mentioned above. One can indeed make the inference from the command premiss

$$[- \ ! \ \text{doing} \ A / \text{you do} \ B]$$

to the command conclusion

$$[- \ ! \ \text{not doing} \ B / \text{you do not do} \ A]$$

Thus the argument

> *X*, whenever (i.e., on any day that) you don't eat eggs for breakfast, eat eggs for lunch!!
> ---
> *X*, whenever you don't eat eggs for lunch, eat eggs for breakfast!!

is valid. But the inference from the premiss

$$[- \ ! \ \text{doing} \ A / B \ \text{occurs}]$$

to the conclusion

$$[- \ ! \ \text{not occurring} \ B / \text{you do not do} \ A]$$

110

is not admissible unless the occurrence of *B* lies within the addressee's power and control. For otherwise the conclusion is nonsensical and ill-formed in that it does not contain a proper command requirement. Thus the 'inference'

X, whenever it rains, take your umbrella!!

X, whenever you do not take your umbrella, it is not to rain [or: 'Do not let it rain']!!

is nonsensical.

*   *   *

It is important to distinguish between the *counter-mand* (negation) of a command and its *withdrawal* or *voiding*[5]. If we withdraw a command, the result is not the issuing of a command at all, but the voiding of the previously issued command which leads — so far as this item is concerned — not to a new command, but to the annihilation of an existing one[6]. The distinction is analogous to that between on the one hand *with-drawing* and on the other *denying* a statement that has been made (asserted).

9.3. Command Fusion. Given two commands *addressed to the same addressee* $C_1 = [X_1 \mathbin{!} A_1/P_1]$ and $C_2 = [X_2 \mathbin{!} A_2/P_2]$ with $X_1 = X_2$, we may define their *fusion* (represented by $\times$) as follows:

$$C_1 \times C_2 = Df \quad [X_1 \mathbin{!} A_1 \mathbin{\&} A_2/P_1 \vee P_2]$$

[5] A distinction between *withdrawing* a command and *counter-manding* it is drawn in *Sellars* (1963), pp. 199–200.

[6] An interesting discussion of command negation, drawing some (but not all) of the pertinent distinctions, is found in *Bergström* (1962*b*), pp. 22–32.

It should be noted that the fusion-command $C_1 \times C_2$ covers each of the commands it fuses. Two consequences immediately follow from this definition:

(1) In general we have it that all of the following inferences are valid (whenever C_1 and C_2 have the same addressee, so that $C_1 \times C_2$ is defined):

$$\frac{C_1 \times C_2}{C_1} \qquad \frac{C_1 \times C_2}{C_2} \qquad \frac{C_1 \times C_2}{C_2 \times C_1}$$

(2) If either $A_1 = A_2$ or $P_1 = P_2$, then the following inference is valid (provided that C_1 and C_2 have the same addressee, so that $C_1 \times C_2$ is defined):

$$\frac{\begin{array}{c} C_1 \\ C_2 \end{array}}{C_1 \times C_2}$$

It is not, however, true *in general* that $C_1 \times C_2$ can be inferred from the pair C_1, C_2 even when these have the same addressee. For if

$C_1 = $ [Tom ! close the window/it is raining]

$C_2 = $ [Tom ! close the door/the wind is blowing]

then the fused command $C_1 \times C_2$ has it that Tom is to close the door when it is raining and to close the window when the wind is blowing, neither of which instructions is embodied in the original pair of commands.

In general, whenever the inference from C_1 to C_2 is valid, then so is the inference from $C_1 \times C_3$ to C_2, for any arbitrary command C_3 for which this fusion command is defined.

The inference

$$\frac{C_1{}^* = [X ! A/P]}{(C_1 \times C_2)^*}$$

112

— analogous to that from $\sim p$ to $\sim (p \,\&\, q)$ — is necessarily valid for any command C_2 for which $C_1 \times C_2$ is defined.

9.4. Command Disjunction. Given the command requirements $A_1, A_2, \ldots, A_n$ it is possible — and indeed important — to distinguish between

(1) The complex *choice-presenting* command requirement, to be symbolized '$\dot{\text{v}} (A_1, A_2, \ldots, A_n)$', which requires realization of *at least one of the* A_i *to be chosen indifferently from the entire group*[7]

and

(2) The complex *alternative-indicating* command requirement to be symbolized '$\bar{\text{v}} (A_1, A_2, \ldots, A_n)$', which requires realization of *certain (and so at least one) of the* A_i— *not to be selected indifferently but* — *to be identified with a view to 'other considerations' which single out one or more of the* A_i *as the 'appropriate' alternatives.*

Correspondingly, given two commands *addressed to the same recipient and operative under the same execution preconditions*, say $C_1 = [X \,!\, A_1/P]$ and $C_2 = [X \,!\, A_2/P]$, we define two corresponding modes of choice-presenting and alternative-indicating command disjunction:

$$C_1 \,\dot{\text{v}}\, C_2 \;=\; [X \,!\, \dot{\text{v}} \,(A_1, A_2)/P]$$
$$C_1 \,\bar{\text{v}}\, C_2 \;=\; [X \,!\, \bar{\text{v}} \,(A_1, A_2)/P]$$

It is important to note that these modes of disjunction are only defined for a pair of commands in a very special case, viz. that the recipients be the same and

[7] Compare *von Wright* (1963), pp. 158–160.

the execution preconditions be identical.

The command

> X, do either A or B (you are wholly free to choose either one you please, but must do at least one)!

exhibits the special feature of *choice*, which has no obvious analogue in assertoric logic. The command corresponds to the representation

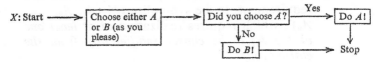

The command has the termination statement: 'X has made a choice between doing (realizing) A and B and has done (realized) the one he chose'. Apart from *requiring the introduction of a somewhat peculiar type of act* — viz. 'acts of choice'—the accommodation of this sort of command imposes no further strains upon the machinery at our disposal[8].

Some examples of disjunctive commands are in order. If a teacher orders the students of a class 'Pupils, write a synopsis either of Hamlet or of Macbeth!' her command is clearly choice-presenting[9]. On the other hand, if she says 'Johnny, do your work quietly or leave the room!' her command is not choice-presenting but alternative-indicating[10].

[8] It will be recalled that choice also entered into commands of the type [X ! A/{P}]. Cf. section 4.4 above.

[9] The situation has no simple assertoric analogue exactly because there is no analogue to *choice* in the domain of assertion or knowledge.

[10] The distinction at issue is, so far as I know, first drawn and exemplified in *Rescher and Robison* (1964).

114

An example of a case in which a disjunctive command is to be construed as alternative-indicating would be a signal from headquarters to a field-unit: 'Execute Order 32! Do not take route (1)!', where Order 32 is 'Set out for objective 365 at 8 a.m. tomorrow along either route (1) or route (2)!'. Another example occurs in the pair of orders:

> Either the door or the window is to be kept open at all times!!

> The door must be kept closed whenever conferences are in progress!!

In both of these examples we have disjunctive commands which are *prima facie* choice-presenting — and which are choice-presenting when 'other things are equal'— but which must *in context* be construed as alternative-indicating.

It should be noted that, while

$$\frac{C_1}{C_1 \, \bar{\text{v}} \, C_2}$$

is a valid mode of command-inference (whenever $C_1 \, \bar{\text{v}} \, C_2$ is defined), the commands

(1) C_1

and

(2) $C_1 \, \dot{\text{v}} \, C_2$

are clearly such that no valid (general) inference from (1) to (2) is possible[11]. We cannot move unproblematically from the command premiss 'Marry Joan!' to the command conclusion 'Marry Joan or marry Mary!'

[11] The termination of a choice-presenting command calls for an actual choice-act in such a way that a scenario may indeed terminate a command C_1 without terminating $C_1 \, \dot{\text{v}} \, C_2$. (See the command program given earlier in this section.)

Failure to draw the requisite distinction has led to much confusion in the discussion of commands and command inferences involving alteration. Already *Mally* (1926) acutely apprehended the nonequivalence of

$$! A \text{ or } ! B \cong \text{Do } A \text{ or do } B!$$

upon the one hand, and

$$! (A \text{ or } B) \cong \text{Do } A \text{ or } B!$$

upon the other[12]. Moreover a rather unprofitable controversy[13] has sprung up — and long continued — over the validity of the inferences

$$\frac{\text{Do } A!}{\text{Do } A \text{ or do } B!} \qquad \frac{\text{Do } A!}{\text{Do } A \text{ or } B!}$$

Thus Ross denies[14] and Hare defends[15] the validity of the command-inferences: 'Slip the letter in the box! Therefore: Slip the letter in the box or burn it!' Our position on the matter is straightforward:

(1) $! A$ or $! B$ (Do A! or Do B!) is *not* a command. The bare disjunction of two commands — whatever this may be — is not a well-formed command.

(2) The inference pattern

$$\frac{\text{Do } A ! \cong [- ! A/(*)]}{\text{Do } A \text{ or } B ! \cong [- ! A \text{ v } B/(*)]}$$

is valid if the disjunctive command conclusion is construed in the (in the case in hand

---

[12] See the discussion in *Menger* (1939), p. 58, where it is rightly stressed that Mally did not utilize this insight properly.

[13] Described in *Bergström* (1962*b*), p. 40.

[14] *Ross* (1944), p. 38. Cf. also *Williams* (1963).

[15] *Hare* (1949).

admittedly artificial) alternative-indicating mode, but is definitely invalid if it is construed as choice-presenting.

In a sense, an alternative-indicating command is not actually complete, since it requires some extrinsic, supplementary information to rule out the 'extraneous' alternatives. Once these have been eliminated, the residual command will be either choice-presenting or altogether non-disjunctive (should only a single alternative be left). This process of 'reducing' an alternative-indicating command issues in such valid modes of disjunctive inference as

$$C_1{}^* = [X \mathbin{!} \sim A_1/P]$$
$$\frac{C_1 \mathbin{\bar{\mathrm{v}}} C_2 = [X \mathbin{!} A_1 \mathbin{\bar{\mathrm{v}}} A_2/P]}{C_2 = [X \mathbin{!} A_2/P]}$$

Thus the disagreement between Hare[16] and Peters[17] over the validity of the inference 'Use an axe or a saw, Don't use an axe, Therefore: Use a saw!' is also to be resolved in line with this distinction. For the inference pattern

$$[- \mathbin{!} A \mathbin{\mathrm{v}} B/(*)]$$
$$\frac{[- \mathbin{!} \sim A/(*)]}{[- \mathbin{!} B/(*)]}$$

is clearly valid if the disjunction of the first premiss is construed as alternative-indicating, whereas the premisses are actually inconsistent when 'v' is read as choice-presenting.

[16] *Hare* (1949), pp. 32–33.
[17] *Peters* (1949), p. 540. Cf. *Bergström* (1962*b*) p. 40.

Consider the patently valid inference

$$C_1 = X, \text{do neither } A \text{ nor } B \text{ !} \cong [X \text{ !} \sim A \text{ \&}$$
$$\sim B/(*)]$$
$$\overline{C_2 = X, \text{do not do } A \text{ !} \cong [X \text{ !} \sim A/(*)]}$$

In view of the considerations adduced above in connection with command-negation, the validity of this inference underwrites antilogistically the validity of

$$C_2{}^* = X, \text{do } A \text{!} \cong [X \text{ !} A/(*)]$$
$$\overline{C_1{}^* = X, \text{do either } A \text{ or } B \text{!} \cong [X \text{ !} A \text{ v } B/(*)]}$$

But is the 'v' of the conclusion here to be construed as 'v̇' or as 'v̄'? Here the resolution clearly has to be made in favour of the alternative-indicating — and *not* the choice-presenting — mode of disjunction.

It would seem plausible to take the alternative-indicating type of command as basic, introducing the choice-presenting type by its means. A choice-presenting command could be construed as a complex consisting of an alternative-indicating command together with certain *authorizations* (cf. p. 105 above). Specifically, the command $C_1 \dot{\text{v}} C_2 = [X \text{ !} A_1 \dot{\text{v}} A_2/P]$ would, on this approach, be regarded as a complex with three constituents:

$$C_1 \bar{\text{v}} C_2 = [X \text{ !} A_1 \bar{\text{v}} A_2/P], \text{ and } (X : A_1/P),$$
$$\text{and } (X : A_2/P)$$

Chapter Ten

COMMAND PROVISOS

10.1. The Concept of a Command Proviso. A command whose execution precondition involves a 'but only' rider (explicitly or by appropriate reconstrual) will be said to contain a *proviso*. Such commands conform to the type 'Do ... but only on condition that ...'. Examples of such commands are:

(i) Whenever (or: 'when next') P is the case, do A but only after first doing B!

(ii) Do A right away, but only after you have first done B!

(iii) Do A whenever you do B, but only then!

(iv) Do A whenever P is the case, but only then!

Every such command amounts to *a pair of linked commands*. Thus (i) amounts — in its 'whenever' version — to the pair of commands:

(i′) $\begin{cases} [- \text{ ! doing } B \text{ and then } A/P] \\ [- \text{ ! } \sim A/P \text{ and you have not first done } B] \end{cases}$

The appropriateness of this analysis is rendered apparent by an examination of the discrete representation of (i), namely:

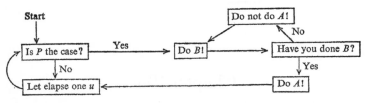

Similarly, commands (ii)–(iv) amount respectively to the pairs:

(ii') $\left\{ \begin{array}{l} [- \; ! \text{ doing } B \text{ and then } A/(*)] \\ [- \; ! \sim A/\text{You have not yet done } B] \end{array} \right.$

(iii') $\left\{ \begin{array}{l} [- \; ! \; A/\text{You do } B] \\ [- \; ! \sim A/\text{You do not do } B] \end{array} \right.$

(iv') $\left\{ \begin{array}{l} [- \; ! \; A/P] \\ [- \; ! \sim A/\sim P] \end{array} \right.$

In each such case, the second command will be said to be a *proviso* to the first.

It should be remarked that 'Do A only when P is the case!!' amounts to the ordinary, proviso-less command

$$[- \; ! \sim A/\sim P]$$

whereas 'Do A, but only when P is the case!!' yields the provisoed command:

$$[- \; ! \; A/P] \text{ subject to } [- \; ! \sim A/\sim P]$$

10.2. Inference from Provisoed Commands. To indicate that the command C_2 is attached as a proviso to the command C_1 we shall write

$$C_1 \; \S \; C_2$$

As regards the validity of command inferences whose premisses involve provisos, we take our cue from the purely assertoric case. Compare the inferences

Command Provisos

p provided that q	p provided that q
$p \supset r$	r provided that s
r provided that q	p and r provided that q, s

Note that here the provisos are simply superimposed on an otherwise valid inference by making the conclusion subject to all the provisos of all of the (essential) premisses[1]. Correspondingly we stipulate:

A command inference whose premisses involve provisos is valid if (i) the corresponding proviso-denuded command inference is valid, and (ii) the conclusion command is made subject to all the provisos of the (essential) premisses[2].

Provisos must be 'carried along' in command inference. We cannot go from the command premiss 'Enter the house, but only after securing the owner's permission!' to the (unqualified) command conclusion 'Enter the house!'

In line with this stipulation, the inference from the command premiss 'Do A and B, but only after you have first done C!' (i.e., 'Do A and B and C, but be sure to do C before doing either A or B!') to the conclusion 'Do A!' is invalid, but either of the conclusions 'Do A, but refrain from doing A (and B too) until after you have first done C!' or even 'Do C!' can validly be

[1] Note, however, that in the purely assertoric case '$p \S q$' can be rendered '$q \supset p$'. This has no analogue with commands, any more than it does in such *modal* cases as 'p is necessary provided q' and 'p is probable provided that q'.

[2] Thus the inference from the command premisses C_1 and $C_2 \S C_3$ to the conclusion C_1 is valid despite the presence of a proviso in the premisses because the provisoed premiss is not needed in validating the inference.

121

inferred from this premiss. For the command at issue is rendered as the pair

$$\left\{ \begin{array}{l} [-\ !\ C/(*)] \\ [-\ !\ A\ \&\ B/(*)]\ \S\ [-\ !\ \sim A\ \&\ \sim B/\text{you have} \\ \quad \text{not done } C] \end{array} \right.$$

It should be noted that, in general, that if C_1 entails C_2 (i.e., whenever the command inference from C_1 as premiss to C_2 as conclusion is valid), then the inferences

$$\frac{C_1\ \S\ C_3}{C_2\ \S\ C_3} \qquad\qquad \frac{C_3\ \S\ C_2}{C_3\ \S\ C_1}$$

will be valid for any C_3 that is compatible with C_1.[3] This is to say that a proviso-qualified command can always be weakened and a command proviso can always be strengthened, other things being equal. These rules too come by analogy with the assertoric case.

In line with these principles, the theory of inference of commands with provisos can be accommodated within the framework of an adequate conception of inference for straightforward, proviso-less commands.

---

[3] The last-named qualification is needed to circumvent acceptance as valid of such an inference as:

$$\frac{[X\ !\ A/P\ \&\ Q]\ \S\ [X\ !\ \sim A/P\ \&\ \sim Q]}{[X\ !\ A/P\ \&\ Q]\ \S\ [X\ !\ \sim A/P]}$$

(I owe this example to Mr. Bas van Fraassen.)

Chapter Eleven

CONCLUSION

It was remarked at the outset in our Introduction that few problem-questions in the logic of commands have as yet been settled by a general consensus. The imperfect considerations of the present volume — whose non-exhaustiveness is plainly attested by the open problems left in our inconclusive treatment of validity in the case of heterogeneous command inference — have certainly not solved all the difficulties arising in this domain. There are, however, three features of the present approach to command logic on which I have sufficient confidence that I should like in concluding to stress them by way of prolegomena to some more finished future theory of commands:

1. The logical analysis of commands should take careful and explicit account of temporal considerations, and an adequate logic of commands will have to be developed in close conjunction with a logic of chronological propositions (a 'tense logic').

2. The pivotal idea of validity in command inference should be construed (in the homogeneous case) in terms of the question of whether the

conclusion command is tacitly or implicitly contained in the 'set of instructions' presented by the command premisses.

3. The semantical theory of validity in command inference, although distinctive and in some ways *sui generis*, is not primitive and self-subsistent, but should be approached from the direction of assertoric logic *via* the bridging-link of statements of command termination (or command 'satisfaction' in some cognate sense).

The considerations put forward here represent but a small step in the development of a comprehensive logical theory of commands that can deserve to meet with general acceptance. We shall regard our labours as amply rewarded if they succeed in convincing the reader that such a theory is at least possible, and in securing to some degree his assent to our general approach towards the direction in which a systematic realization of this possibility lies.

BIBLIOGRAPHY

Preliminary Remarks on the Literature of the 'Logic of Commands'

Mally (1926) must be recognized as a pioneering effort of outstanding merit. Among the older (pre-1945) discussions, four deserve to be ranked as making especially significant contributions: Jørgensen (1937–38), Hofstadter and McKinsey (1939), Menger (1939), and Ross (1941). Hare (1952) has been especially influential in stimulating interest in command-logic in Anglo-American circles. The first monographic survey of our subject is Bergström (1962b), and the present work is indebted to this synoptic treatment at several points. Von Wright (1963) is outstanding among recent works in the field. And in general, one of the noteworthy aspects of the subject is the prominence of Scandinavian contributors after its initial Germanic phase (from Brentano to Mally).

Note: This bibliography is restricted to the 'logic of commands' as such and does not deal with *deontic* logic. For the literature of this field see A. R. Anderson, *The Formal Analysis of Normative Systems* (New Haven, 1956). A reference is given to the review of each item in the *Journal of Symbolic Logic* (cited as JSL) whenever possible.

Bibliography

The Literature

PRANTL (1855). Carl Prantl. *Geschichte der Logik im Abendlande*, vol. 1 (Leipzig, 1855). [On Stoic discussions of commands, see pp. 441–442. Cf. B. Mates *Stoic Logic* (Berkeley and Los Angeles, 1953), p. 19.]

BRENTANO (1889). Franz Clemens Brentano. *Vom Ursprung sittlicher Erkenntnis*. Leipzig, 1889. 2d edition by O. Kraus, Leipzig, 1902. [Ultimate source of the Husserl–Meinong–Wolff–Mally line of development.]

FREGE (1892). Gottlob Frege. 'Ueber Sinn und Bedeutung.' *Zeitschrift für Philosophie und philosophische Kritik*, vol. 100 (1892), pp. 25–50. [On commands see pp. 38–39. English translation in *Philosophical Writings of Gottlob Frege* by P. Geach and M. Black (Oxford, 1952), see p. 68. On Frege's theory of commands see Rulon S. Wells, 'Frege's Ontology', *The Review of Metaphysics*, vol. 4 (1950–1951), pp. 537–573 (see pp. 557–558).]

SIGWART (1895). Christoph Sigwart. *Logic*, vol. 1. Tr. by H. Dendy, London, 1895 (from the 2d ed. of 1888; 1st ed., 1873). [On commands see especially pp. 17–18.]

HUSSERL (1901). Edmund Husserl. *Logische Untersuchungen*. Leipzig, 1913, 1922. [On commands see vol. 2, § 68, p. 679.]

MEINONG (1902). Alexis Meinong. *Ueber Annahmen*. Leipzig, 1902; 2d edition, 1910. [On commands see §§ 40, 47, 52, *et passim*.]

Bibliography

ERDMANN (1907). Benno Erdmann. *Logik*, vol. 1, Halle a.S., 1907. [For commands see the index s.v. 'Befehle'.]

MAIER (1908). Heinrich Maier. *Die Psychologie des emotiven Denkens*. Tübingen, 1908. [On commands see pp. 371 and 616 ff.]

POINCARÉ (1913). Henri Poincaré. 'La Morale et la Science.' *Dernières Pensées*. Paris (Flammarion). 1913, pp. 223–247.

MOORE (1914). G. E. Moore. *Ethics*. Oxford, 1914, [See Chapter IV.]

MEINONG (1917). Alexis Meinong. 'Ueber emotionale Präsentation.' *Sitzungsberichte der kaiserlichen Akademie der Wissenschaften in Wien*, vol. 183 (1917).

MEINONG (1923). Alexis Meinong. *Zur Grundlegung der allgemeinen Werttheorie*. Herausgegeben von E. Mally. Graz, 1923.

WOLFF (1924). Karl Wolff. *Grundlehre des Sollens*. Innsbruck, 1924.

MALLY (1926). Ernst Mally. *Grundgesetze des Sollens: Elemente der Logik des Willens*. Graz, 1926.

MENGER (1934). Karl Menger. *Moral, Wille, und Weltgestaltung: Grundlegung der Logik der Sitten*. Wien, 1934.

CARNAP (1935). Rudolf Carnap. *Philosophy and Logical Syntax*. London, 1935. [See section 4 of Chapter I.]

DUBISLAV (1937). Walter Dubislav. 'Zur Unbegründbarkeit der Forderungssätze.' *Theoria*, vol. 3 (1937), pp. 330–342.

Bibliography

JØRGENSEN (1937–1938). Jørgen Jørgensen. 'Imperatives and Logic.' *Erkenntnis*, vol. 7 (1937–1938), pp. 288–296. [Reviewed by C. A. Baylis in JSL, vol. 4 (1939), p. 36.]

JØRGENSEN (1938). Jørgen Jørgensen. 'Imperativer og Logik.' *Theoria*, vol. 4 (1938), pp. 183–190.

GRELLING (1939). Kurt Grelling. 'Zur Logik der Sollsätze.' *Unity of Science Forum*, January, 1939, pp. 44–47. [Reviewed by Frederic B. Fitch in JSL, vol. 5 (1940), p. 39.]

GRUE-SØRENSEN (1939). K. Grue-Sørensen. 'Imperativsätze und Logik. Begegnung einer Kritik.' *Theoria*, vol. 5 (1939), pp. 195–202. [Reviewed by Frederic B. Fitch in JSL, vol. 5 (1940), pp. 40–41.]

HOFSTADTER AND MCKINSEY (1939). Albert Hofstadter and J. C. C. McKinsey. 'On the Logic of Imperatives.' *Philosophy of Science*, vol. 6 (1939), pp. 446–457. [Reviewed by Frederic B. Fitch in JSL, vol. 5 (1940), p. 41.]

MENGER (1939). Karl Menger. 'A Logic of the Doubtful: On Optative and Imperative Logic.' *Reports of a Mathematical Colloquium* (Notre Dame University (Indiana), University Press), second series, No. 1 (1939), pp. 53–64. [Reviewed by Frederic B. Fitch in JSL, vol. 5 (1940), p. 40.]

RAND (1939). Rose Rand. 'Logik der Forderungssätze.' *Internationale Zeitschrift für Theorie des Rechtes*, vol. 1 (1939), pp. 308–322. [Reviewed by Frederic B. Fitch in JSL, vol. 5 (1940), pp. 41–42.]

Bibliography

REACH (1939). Karl Reach. 'Some Comments on Grelling's paper "Zur Logik der Sollsaetze".' *Unity of Science Forum*, April, 1939, p. 72. [Reviewed by Frederic B. Fitch in JSL, vol. 5 (1940), p. 39.]

SORAINEN (1939). Kalle Sorainen. 'Der Modus und die Logik.' *Theoria*, vol. 5 (1939), pp. 202–204.

HEDENIUS (1941). I. Hedenius. *Om rätt och moral.* Stockholm, 1941.

ROSS (1941). Alf Ross. 'Imperatives and Logic.' *Theoria*, vol. 7 (1941), pp. 53–71. [Reviewed by C. G. Hempel in JSL, vol. 6 (1941), pp. 105–106.]

VARTIOVAARA (1941). Klaus V. Vartiovaara. 'Logic and Ethics' (in Finnish). *Ajatus*, vol. 10 (1941), pp. 285–300. [Reviewed by G. H. von Wright in JSL, vol. 7 (1942), p. 43.]

LEDENT (1942). Adrien Ledent. 'Le statut logique des propositions imperatives.' *Theoria*, vol. 8 (1942), pp. 262–271.

ALDRICH (1943). V. C. Aldrich. 'Do Commands Express Propositions?' *Journal of Philosophy*, vol. 40 (1943), pp. 654–657.

BEARDSLEY (1944). Elizabeth L. Beardsley. 'Imperative Sentences in Relation to Indicatives.' *Philosophical Review*, vol. 53 (1944), pp. 175–185. [Reviewed by J. Kraft in JSL, vol. 9 (1944), pp. 48–49.]

OPPENHEIM (1944). Felix E. Oppenheim. 'Outline of a Logical Analysis of Law.' *Philosophy of Science*, vol. 11 (1944), pp. 142–160. [Reviewed by N. Goodman in JSL, vol. 9 (1944), pp. 105–106.]

ROSS (1944). Alf Ross. 'Imperatives and Logic.' *Philosophy of Science*, vol. 11 (1944), pp. 30–46. [Reviewed by A. Church in JSL, vol. 9 (1944), p. 48.]

SAARNIO (1944). Uuno Saarnio. 'Value and Ethics' (in Finnish). *Ajatus*, vol. 13 (1944), pp. 113–235. [Reviewed by H. Kinos in JSL, vol. 10 (1945), p. 130.]

STEVENSON (1944). C. L. Stevenson. *Ethics and Language*. New Haven, 1944.

BOHNERT (1945). Herbert G. Bohnert. 'The Semiotic Status of Commands.' *Philosophy of Science*, vol. 12 (1945), pp. 302–315. [Reviewed by Frederic B. Fitch in JSL, vol. 11 (1946), p. 98.]

SEGERSTEDT (1945). T. T. Segerstedt. 'Imperative Propositions and Judgments of Value.' *Theoria*, vol. 11 (1945), pp. 1–19.

SIMON (1945). Herbert A. Simon. *Administrative Behavior*. New York, 1945; 2d edition, 1957. [On commands see especially chapter III, 'Fact and Value in Decision-making.']

LEWIS (1946). C. I. Lewis. *An Analysis of Knowledge and Valuation*. La Salle, Illinois, 1946. [On commands see the Index s.v. 'Imperative'.]

MORRIS (1946). Charles Morris. *Signs, Language, and Behavior*. New York, 1946. [See especially pp. 83–86.]

STORER (1946). Thomas Storer. 'The Logic of Value Imperatives.' *Philosophy of Science*, vol. 13 (1946), pp. 25–40. [Reviewed by C. G. Hempel in JSL, vol. 11 (1946), pp. 97–98.]

Bibliography

BETH (1946–1947). E. W. Beth. 'On a Possible Interpretation of Imperatives.' *Synthese*, vol. 5 (1946–1947), pp. 94–95.

EWING (1947). A. C. Ewing. *The Definition of the Good.* London and New York, 1947. [See chapters I and IV.]

REICHENBACH (1947). Hans Reichenbach. *Elements of Symbolic Logic.* New York, 1947. (See § 57.) [Reviewed by G. W. Berry in JSL, vol. 14 (1949), p. 50.]

POPPER (1948). Karl Popper. 'What can Logic do for Philosophy?' *Proceedings of the Aristotelian Society* Supplementary Volume 22 (1948), pp. 141–154.

SAARNIO (1948). Uuno Saarnio. 'Der Begriff des Guten.' *Theoria*, vol. 14 (1948), pp. 68–83.

TAMMELO (1948). Ilmar Tammelo. *Legal Dogmatics and the Mathesis Universalis.* Heidelberg, 1948. Reprinted in *idem.*, *Drei rechtsphilosophische Aufsätze.* (Heidelberg, 1948.)

HARE (1949). R. M. Hare. 'Imperative Sentences.' *Mind,* vol. 58 (1949), pp. 21–39. [Reviewed by J. C. C. McKinsey in JSL, vol. 15 (1950), p. 145.]

PARADIES (1949). Fritz Paradies. 'Die Konformationsregeln der empirischen Rechtswissenschaft.' *Methodos*, vol. 1 (1949), pp. 256–269; English version, pp. 270–276. [Reviewed by Frederic B. Fitch in JSL, vol. 17 (1952), p. 61.]

PETERS (1949). A. F. Peters. 'R. M. Hare on Imperative Sentences: A Criticism.' *Mind,* vol. 58 (1949), pp. 535–540. [Reviewed by J. C. C. McKinsey in JSL, vol. 15 (1950), p. 145.]

Bibliography

PRIOR (1949). Arthur N. Prior. *Logic and the Basis of Ethics*. Oxford, 1949. [See Chapter VII and Note B in the Appendix.]

FIELD (1950). G. C. Field. 'Note on Imperatives.' *Mind*, vol. 59 (1950), pp. 230–232. [A critique of *Hare* (1949).]

STRAWSON (1950). P. F. Strawson. 'Truth.' *Proceedings of the Aristotelian Society*, Supplementary Volume 24 (1950). Reprinted in G. Pitcher (ed.), *Truth* (Englewood Cliffs, N.J., 1964).

COSSIO (1951). Carlos Cossio. 'Las posibilidades de la lógica juridíca según la lógica de Husserl.' *Revista de la Facultad de Derecho, Buenos Aires*, vol. 23 (1951), pp. 201–241. [Re-issued with addition as 'La norma y el imperativo en Husserl.' *Revista brasiliera de filosofia*, vol. 10 (1960), pp. 43–90.]

HARE (1951). R. M. Hare. 'An Examination of *The Place of Reason in Ethics* by S. E. Toulmin.' *Philosophical Quarterly*, vol. 1 (1951), pp. 372–375.

VON WRIGHT (1951). G. H. von Wright. 'Deontic Logic.' *Mind*, vol. 60 (1951), pp. 1–15. [Reviewed by Frederic B. Fitch in JSL, vol. 17 (1952), p. 140.]

DUNCAN-JONES (1952). A. E. Duncan-Jones. 'Assertions and Commands.' *Proceedings of the Aristotelian Society*, vol. 52 (1952), pp. 189–206.

HALL (1952). Everett W. Hall. *What is Value? An Essay in Philosophical Analysis*. New York 1952, and London 1952, xi + 255 pp. [Chapter 6 is especially relevant to imperatives. Reviewed (together with articles by Herbert Hochberg, E. W.

Bibliography

Hall, and E. M. Adams) by Romane Clark in JSL, Vol. 24 (1959), pp. 89–91; and by R. M. Hare in *Mind*, vol. 58 (1954), pp. 262–269.]

HARE (1952). R. M. Hare. *The Language of Morals.* Oxford, 1952; reprinted 1961. [Reviewed by R. B. Braithwaite in *Mind*, vol. 58 (1954), pp. 249–262.]

HEDENIUS (1952). I. Hedenius. 'Hpothetiska befall-ningar.' ['Hypothetical imperatives.'] *Ajatus*, vol. 17 (1952), pp. 49–77.

VON WRIGHT (1952). G. H. von Wright. 'On the Logic of Some Axiological and Epistemological Concepts.' *Ajatus*, vol. 17 (1952), pp. 213–234. [Reviewed by A. R. Anderson in JSL, vol. 19 (1954), pp. 133–134.]

FALK (1953). W. D. Falk. 'Goading and Guiding.' *Mind*, vol. 62 (1953), pp. 145–171.

KALINOVSKI (1953). Jerzy Kalinovski. 'Théorie des propositions normatives.' *Studia Logica*, vol. 1 (1953), pp. 147–182.

CASTANEDA (1954). Hector Neri Castaneda. 'Logica de las normans y la etica.' *Universidad de San Carlos, Guatemala*, vol. 30 (1954), pp. 129–196. [Reviewed by G. Stahl in JSL, vol. 22 (1957), pp. 388–389.]

NOWELL-SMITH (1954). P. H. Nowell-Smith. *Ethics.* London, 1954.

PRIOR (1954). A. N. Prior. 'The Paradoxes of Derived Obligation.' *Mind*, vol. 63 (1954), pp. 49–63. [Reviewed by N. Rescher in JSL, vol. 19 (1954), p. 133.]

TURNBULL (1954). R. G. Turnbull. 'A Note on Mr Hare's "Logic of Imperatives".' *Philosophical Studies*, vol. 5 (1954), pp. 33–35. [Reviewed by A. N. Prior in JSL, vol. 23 (1958), p. 442.]

Bibliography

CASTANEDA (1955). Hector Neri Castaneda. 'A Note on Imperative Logic.' *Philosophical Studies*, vol. 6 (1955), pp. 1–4. [Reviewed by G. Stahl in JSL, vol. 24 (1959), pp. 87–88.]

EDWARDS (1955). Paul Edwards. *The Logic of Moral Discourse*. Glencoe, 1955. [See chapter VI.]

HEDENIUS (1955). I. Hedenius. 'Befallningssatzer, normer och värdentsagor.' *Moderne Vienskab, Orientering og Debat*, Nordisk Sommerunwersitet 1954 (København, 1955), pp. 178–202.

SELLARS (1956). Wilfrid Sellars. 'Imperatives, Intentions, and the Logic of "Ought".' *Methodos*, vol. 8 (1956), pp. 227–268; reprinted in an expanded form in *Morality and the Language of Conduct* ed. by H. Castaneda and G. Nakhnikian (Detroit, Wayne University Press, 1963).

VISALBERGHI (1956–1958). Aldo Visalberghi. 'Forma logica e contenuto empirico negli enunciati valutativi. I — La logica degli imperativi e delle norme.' *Rivista di filosofia*, vol. 47 (1956), pp. 424–453. *Idem.*, 'II — Valuatzione e "transazione",' *ibid.*, vol. 48 (1957), pp. 382–415, and vol. 49 (1958), pp. 38–68. Re-issued in the author's book *Esperienza e valuatzione* (Torino, 1958).

CASTANEDA (1957). Hector Neri Castaneda. 'Un Sistema general de logica normativa.' *Dianoia* (Mexico) vol. 2 (1957), pp. 303–333. [Reviewed by G. Stahl in JSL, vol. 22 (1957), pp. 388–389.]

MAYO AND MITCHELL (1957). Bernard Mayo and Basil Mitchell. 'The Varieties of Imperative.' *Proceedings of the Aristotelian Society* Supplementary Volume 31 (1957), pp. 161–190.

Bibliography

WEINBERGER (1957). Ota Weinberger. 'Über die Negation von Sollsätzen.' *Theoria*, vol. 23 (1957), pp. 102–132.

CASTANEDA (1958). Hector Neri Castaneda. 'Imperatives and Deontic Logic.' *Analysis*, vol. 19 (1958), pp. 42–48. [Reviewed by J. Bennett in JSL, vol. 24 (1959), pp. 264–265.]

DUMMETT (1958). Michael Dummett. 'Truth.' *Proceedings of the Aristotelian Society*, vol. 59 (1958–1959). Reprinted in G. Pitcher (ed.) *Truth* (Englewood Cliffs, N.J., 1964).

GEACH (1958). Peter Thomas Geach. 'Imperative and Deontic Logic.' *Analysis*, vol. 18 (1958), pp. 49–56. [Reviewed by J. Bennett in JSL, vol. 24 (1959), pp. 264–265.]

WEINBERGER (1958). Ota Weinberger. *Die Sollsatzproblematik in der modernen Logik: Können Sollsätze (Imperative) als wahr bezeichnet werden?* Prague ('Rozpravy Ceskoslovenské Akademie Ved', Rada Spolecenskych Ved, vol. 68, 1958, No. 9), 1958. Pp. 161.

ZINOV'EV (1958). A. A. Zinov'ev. 'O logike normativnyh predlozenij' ('The logic of normative propositions'). *Voprosy filozofij*, no. 1 (1958), pp. 156–159.

JUAREZ-PAZ (1959). Rigoberto Juarez-Paz. 'Reasons, Commands, and Moral Principles.' *Logique et Analyse*, vol. 2 (1959), pp. 194–205.

LEONARD (1959). Henry S. Leonard. 'Interrogatives, Imperatives, Truth, Falsity, and Lies.' *Philosophy of Science*, vol. 26 (1959), pp. 172–186.

Bibliography

TAMMELO (1959). Ilmar Tammelo. 'On the Logical Openness of Legal Orders: A Modal Analysis of Law with Special Reference to the Logical Status of *Non licet* in International Law.' *The American Journal of Comparative Law*, vol. 8 (1959), pp. 187–203.

CASTANEDA (1960). Hector Neri Castaneda. 'Outline of a Theory on the General Logical Structure of the Language of Action.' *Theoria*, vol. 26 (1960), pp. 151–182.

GIBBONS (1960). P. C. Gibbons. 'Imperatives and Indicatives.' *Australasian Journal of Philosophy*, vol. 38 (1960), pp. 107–119 and 207–217.

MORRIS (1960). Herbert Morris. 'Imperatives and Orders.' *Theoria*, vol. 26 (1960), pp. 183–209.

TURNBULL (1960). R. G. Turnbull. 'Imperatives, Logic and Moral Obligation.' *Philosophy of Science*, vol. 27 (1960), pp. 374–390.

WEINBERGER (1960). Ota Weinberger. *Studie k logice normativnich vet* ('Studies on the logic of normative propositions'). Prague ('Rozpravy Ceskoslovenské Akademie Ved', Rada Spolecenskych Ved, vol. 70, 1960, No. 1), 1960. Pp. 67.

CASTANEDA (1960–1961). Hector Neri Castaneda. 'Imperative Reasonings.' *Philosophy and Phenomenological Research*, vol. 21 (1960–1961), pp. 21–49.

DOWNING (1961). P. B. Downing. 'Opposite Conditionals and Deontic Logic.' *Mind*, vol. 70 (1961), pp. 491–502.

136

Bibliography

FISHER (1961). Mark Fisher. 'A Logical Theory of Commanding.' *Logique et Analyse*, vol. 4 (1961), pp. 154–169.

MCGUIRE (1961). M. C. McGuire. 'Can I do what I think I ought not?' *Mind*, vol. 70 (1961), pp. 400–404. [A critique of *Hare* (1952).]

WELLMAN (1961). Carl Wellman. *The Language of Ethics*. Cambridge, Mass., 1961.

BERGSTRÖM (1962a). Lars Bergström. 'Comments on Castaneda's Semantics of Prescriptive Discourse.' *Theoria*, vol. 28 (1962), pp. 70–72.

BERGSTRÖM (1962b). Lars Bergström. *Imperatives and Ethics*. Stockholm: Stockholm University, 1962; 98 pp.

CASTANEDA (1962a). Hector Neri Castaneda. 'A Logico–Metaphysical Inquiry into the Language of Action.' *Morality and the Language of Conduct*, ed. by G. Nakhnikian and H. Castaneda, Detroit, Wayne University Press, 1962; pp. 219–301.

CASTANEDA (1962b). Hector Neri Castaneda. 'The Semantics of Prescriptive Discourse.' *Theoria*, vol. 28 (1962), pp. 72–78. [A reply to *Bergström* (1962a).]

FISHER (1962). Mark Fisher. 'A System of Deontic-Alethic Modal Logic.' *Mind*, vol. 71 (1962), pp. 231–236. [Reviewed by H. N. Castaneda in JSL, vol. 27 (1962), pp. 220–221.]

LEMMON (1962). E. J. Lemmon. 'Moral Dilemmas.' *Philosophical Review*, vol. 71 (1962), pp. 139–158.

Bibliography

CHISHOLM (1963). Roderick Chisholm. 'Contrary-to-Duty Imperatives and Deontic Logic.' *Analysis*, vol. 24 (1963), pp. 33–36.

CURRY (1963). Haskell B. Curry. *Foundations of Mathematical Logic*. New York, 1963. [For a discussion of 'Markov algorithms' relating to command sequences in the theory of computation, see pp. 70–80; and for the literature of this subject see p. 84.]

GEACH (1963). Peter Thomas Geach. 'Imperative Inference.' *Analysis Supplement*, 1963 (for vol. 23), pp. 37–42.

HARE (1963). R. M. Hare. *Freedom and Reason*. Oxford, 1963.

SMILEY (1963). T. J. Smiley. 'The Logical Basis of Ethics.' *Acta Philosophica Fennica*, fasc. 16 (1963), pp. 237–246.

WILLIAMS (1963). B. A. O. Williams. 'Imperative Inference.' *Analysis Supplement*, 1963 (for vol. 23), pp. 30–36. [Argues the impossibility of 'inference' among imperatives.]

VON WRIGHT (1963). G. H. von Wright. *Norm and Action*. London and New York, 1963.

ÅQVIST (1964). Lennart Åqvist. 'Interpretations of Deontic Logic.' *Mind*, vol. 73 (1964), pp. 246–253.

LEMMON (1964). John Lemmon. 'Deontic Logic and the Logic of Imperatives.' Paper (to date unpublished) presented at the annual meeting of the Western Division of the American Philosophical Association (Milwaukee, May 1964).

Bibliography

LLEWELYN (1964). John E. Llewelyn. 'What is a Question?' *Australasian Journal of Philosophy*, vol. 42 (1964), pp. 67–85. [Considers *inter alia* the relation between questions and commands. The thesis that questions can be reformulated as imperatives was maintained in *Hare* (1949), p. 24. It goes back to B. Bosanquet: *Logic* (Oxford, 1881), vol. I, pp. 36 and 380 (n. 2); and *Knowledge and Reality* (London, 1885), p. 114.]

RESCHER AND ROBISON (1964). Nicholas Rescher and John Robison. 'Can One Infer Commands from Commands?' *Analysis*, vol. 24 (1964), pp. 176–179. [A critique of *Williams* (1963).]

GOMBAY (1965). André Gombay. 'Imperative Inference and Disjunction.' *Analysis*, vol. 25 (1965), pp. 58–62. [A critique of *Rescher and Robison* (1964).]

ÅQVIST (1965). Lennart Åqvist. 'Choice-Offering and Alternative-Presenting Disjunctive Commands.' *Analysis*, vol. 25 (1965), pp. 182–187. [Defends *Rescher and Robison* (1964) against *Gombay* (1965).]

KEENE (1966). G. B. Keene. 'Can Commands Have Logical Consequences?' *American Philosophical Quarterly*, vol. 3 (1966).

SIMON (1966). Herbert A. Simon. 'The Logic of Rational Decision.' *British Journal for the Philosophy of Science*, vol. 17 (1966).

KANGER (1957). Stig Kanger. *New Foundations for Ethical Theory*. Stockholm, 1957.

INDICES

INDEX OF SYMBOLS

INDEX OF NAMES

Index of Names

142

Index of Names

GENERAL INDEX

143

For Product Safety Concerns and Information please contact our EU
representative GPSR@taylorandfrancis.com Taylor & Francis Verlag GmbH,
Kaufingerstraße 24, 80331 München, Germany

Printed and bound by CPI Group (UK) Ltd, Croydon, CR0 4YY
08/06/2025
01897011-0001